TALES FROM THE KINGDOM OF TONGA

BY
'ILISAPESI LINA WEIR
E. LUTE SISIFA ALEAMOTU'A AND
'ALEKISANITA UINOA-'I-HAKAU F. SISIFA

Tales From the Kingdom of Tonga

Copyright © 2021 by 'Ilisapesi Lina Weir. All rights reserved.

No part of this publication may be reproduced, stored in a retrieval system or transmitted in any way by any means, electronic, mechanical, photocopy, recording or otherwise without the prior permission of the author except as provided by USA copyright law.

The opinions expressed by the author are not necessarily those of URLink Print and Media.

1603 Capitol Ave., Suite 310 Cheyenne, Wyoming USA 82001
1-888-980-6523 | admin@urlinkpublishing.com

URLink Print and Media is committed to excellence in the publishing industry.

Book design copyright © 2021 by URLink Print and Media. All rights reserved.

Published in the United States of America

Library of Congress Control Number: 2020913763
ISBN 978-1-64753-449-3 (Paperback)
ISBN 978-1-64753-450-9 (Digital)

25.11.20

DEDICATION

This book was written by 'Ilisapesi L. Sisifa Weir, 'E. Lute Sisifa Aleamotu'a and 'Alekisanita Uinoa-i-Hakau F. Sisifa in honour of their loving parents Mafi Helu Sisifa and Rev Sione Finau Sisifa.

Contents

Acknowledgements 9

Preamble 11

Chapter 1 13
    Sione Finau Sisifa And
    Mafi Angahiki Helu 13
    Sione Finau Sisifa Of Lofanga, Ha'apai 14
    Sione's Celebratory Kava As Remembered By 82
    Year Old Taumoepenu On June 16, 2004 21
    Mafi Angahiki Helu 23

Chapter 2 32
    1942-1948 Veitongo, Vaipoa, Foa
    Tonga's Involvement
    With World War 11 32
    School At Veitongo 32
    Mafi's Underground Oven 33
    Sione Finau Sisifa's Ordination 36
    Sione's First Posting 36
    Lotofoa In Ha'apai And Hihifo In Niuatotapu 42

Chapter 3 49
    Niuatoputapu 1950-1952 49
    Church Ministry 61

Chapter 4 66
    Kolovai: July 1952 – 1955 66
    Play Time 72

Chapter 5 82
- Houma 1956-1957 82
- Home Life 84
- School Life 89
- Week-End Play 93
- Church Life 94

Chapter 6 96
- Ma'ufanga 1957-1959 96
- School Life 100
- Spare Time 102
- Church & Social Life 102
- Visitors From Ha'apai And Vava'u 107

Chapter 7 109
- Vaini 1960–1962 109
- Education 112
- Home Life 115
- Prize Giving Events: THS and QSC 122

Chapter 8 124
- The Family Unit Breaks Up. 1962 124
- The Story Of The Shipwreck 129
- Mum's Last Months 131
- Devastation After The Burial 133
- Dad's Struggles 135

Chapter 9 140
- Fasi-Moe-Afi 1963–1965 140
- Mosiana's Career In Tonga 141
- Pesi's Short Visit From Auckland 143
- Development Of Lute's Career. 147
- Lute's Major Decision On Her Future 150
- Lute's Future Home 151

    Dad Retires 151
    Maeakafa's Promotions 155

Chapter 10 157
    The Closing Of An Era And The Dawn Of The New 157
    'Alekisanita In Queensland 160
    Lute And Maeakafa's Move To The Police Training
    Academy 162
    Farewelling Our Dad 162
    Sione Finau And Mafi Helu Sisifa's Six Children
    And Their Families, As At January 2018 166
    A Summary Of The Lives Of The Six Sisifa
    Children And Their Families In Early 2018 168
    In Tribute To 'Alekisanita Uinoa-'i-Hakau Fiemano Sisifa 192
    In Memory Of Muni. 198

Chapter 11 200
    Migrations And Ancient Tongan Religion 200
    Christianity Arrived In Tonga 204
    Recollections By Rev Lopeti Taufa 208
    Child Rearing 210
    Short Lives Well Lived 212

Appendices 215
    Figure Listing 215
    Family Tree Listing 225
    Abbreviations 225

Photos 241

ACKNOWLEDGEMENTS

Thank you Mele Moala Aleamotu'a Me'a'ofa for accompanying Lute to interview and document the experiences and memories of many friends and relatives of our parents. Without your records, our book would not have had the depth and insights into the effectiveness or otherwise of our parents' toils. Thank you also for your tireless research of The Free Wesleyan Church of Tonga's Archives for relevant material.

Fig 1. Rev Siupeli and Helen Taliai, 2016.

We would like to thank Helen Ruth Taliai for her tireless and invaluable assistance with reviewing our manuscript, making suggestions from her wealth of knowledge and experience from publishing her own books and those of her husband, Rev Siupeli Taliai. Being an Australian who spent the major part of her life in Tonga, Helen has a deep understanding and perspective of the geography, history and culture of its people. Her parents, Ruth Woodgate and

Rev Ronald (Ron) Woodgate, had many leadership roles in Tonga from 1947 to 1961 in Education and Church Ministry. Rev Woodgate was a President of the Free Wesleyan Church of Tonga.

Many thanks to Sione 'Oleti Taufa for his professional assistance in preparing our manuscript and organising its printing.

Much background material and knowledge was gained from the following publications:

1. *Tupou College Sesquicentenary History (TCSH)* by the team: Rev. Siupeli Taliai, Mrs Helen Taliai, Rev. Dr Geofferey Cummins, Mrs Anne Cummins, Rev. 'Alifeleti'Atiola, Mrs 'Aioema 'Atiola.
2. *History And Geography Of Tonga* by A. H. Wood.
3. *'E ke u 'elelo afe mai!* by Siupeli T. Taliai
4. *Tongan Society At The Time Of Captain Cook's Visits* by Elizabeth Bott and Tavi.
5. *Wikipedia* for maps and various geographical and historical information.

Finally, we would like to thank most sincerely, Retired President of The Free Wesleyan Church of Tonga, Rev Lopeti Taufa, for his insightful summary of our parents' working lives. We are particularly grateful to him because his observations were testimony to exactly what and how we lived at the time. Our recollections of our parent's lives were not merely dreams nor tales. They were, are and will continue to be our reality.

PREAMBLE
JUNE 2004

by 'Alekisanita; Uinoa-'i- Hakau Fiemano Sisifa.

These memoirs are written to complement those of my two sisters in an effort to bring to the fore the loving memories of our parents, Mafi Angahiki Helu Sisifa of Lotofoa and Sione Finau Sisifa of Lofanga, who brought us into this world and raised us in such marvellous ways under extremely trying circumstances. It is a work of love with the hope that future generations arising from our family tree will gain insight into the value systems that made us, the six children of Sione Finau and Mafi Helu Sisifa, what we are.

CHAPTER 1

*"The best and most beautiful things in
the world cannot be seen or even touched
– they must be felt with the heart."*
Helen Keller

SIONE FINAU SISIFA AND MAFI ANGAHIKI HELU

Mafi was woken up by melodic wind-like whispers. She turned over in her bed. The flying foxes that normally screeched in the mornings seemed restrained and whispering with joy today. Light was starting to seep in through her windows. A new and wonderful day was dawning. She thanked God for everything He had given her and asked for His blessings on her special day in 1942.

Neomai stirred. She was very pleased with herself. The handsome young primary school Principal from across the road had proposed to her beautiful young cousin. Today was going to be a perfect day. Neomai thoroughly approved of the match and she would do everything to make this wedding a memorable occassion for her cousin and dear friend. Mafi was a regular visitor here. This time she was on holidays from her teaching job at Queen Sālote College. Ever since Mafi came from Lotofoa to Nuku'alofa to attend QSC, Neomai, had been a constant companion and friend to her. Neomai admitted to herself that she had been casting her eyes around for a suitable husband for Mafi. Sione had caught her eye as a possible husband for her favourite cousin. How wonderful that God works in mysterious ways!

For the rest of the day, there was a quiet excitement in the *'api faifekau* (Minister's residence) of Rev 'Ikani and his wife Neomai Helu Taliai in Kolovai.

Across the road from the *'api faifekau*, was a big weatherboard house, the residence of the principal of the Church Primary School, Sione Finau Sisifa. There was a cool breeze blowing. Sione had found it difficult to go to sleep last night. Many things were going through his mind. Firstly, his gratefulness that his bride-to-be accepted his proposal. He had always admired her from a distance by the way she walked with her back straight and head held high. She was always immaculately dressed. Her long dark straight hair was always swept back tidily. She was slim and always poised. He knew in his heart, mind and soul, that his 'Maker' had chosen this young woman for his partner for the rest of his life.

SIONE FINAU SISIFA OF LOFANGA, HA'APAI

Sione was born in Lofanga to MUNI (Viliami Pulotu) and Uaafe Lua Fehoko in 1914. MUNI is short for Muni-mata-mahae, an inherited title for one of the King's spokespersons, *Matapule of Lofanga*. His family was treated with deference because of the legend of their lineage and their position. The bay where little boats land on the island is named *Fanga ko Lua-a-Muni* (Bay of Muni's Vomit). This little bay is so named because the landing is nearly always very rough, causing people to vomit when landing or hopping into their canoes to take them to land.

Because of its isolation, Lofanga was often used for brutal historical events. According to *History and Geography of Tonga* by A.H. Wood M.A., Finau 'Ulukalala punished the 10 royalists that survived the horrific Civil War of 1799 in Lofanga. He drowned some in leaky canoes and the rest were ordered to be tied to trees and starved to death.

In about 1887, King Tupou 1 and his government formally declared a secession of the Weslyan Church of Tonga from the Australasian Wesleyan Church. Persecution of the Wesleyans who refused to join the Free Wesleyan Church of Tonga began. People of Lofanga were among those whose properties were forcibly possessed and then banished to the Fiji Island of Koro.

There are many versions of the legend of Muni Matamahae, all reinforcing the fact that he had mighty power, like Hercules of the Greek mythology (reminiscent of the Tongan footballer, Lomu, at the Rugby Games in South Africa, running at top speed while waving his opponents aside!) Interesting that Lomu had Lofanga and Foa roots!

HA'APAI ISLANDS

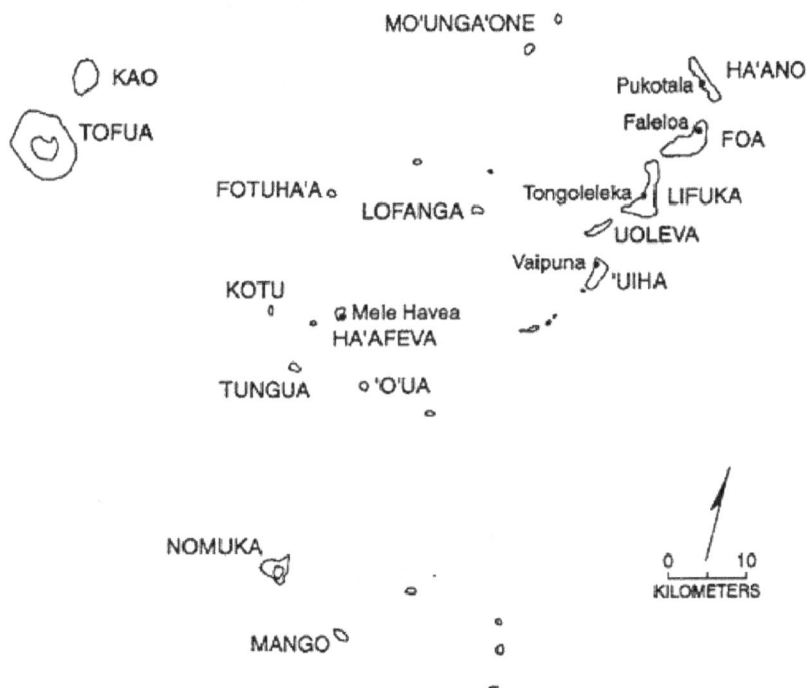

Fig 2. Ha'apai Islands Map

With the last day of term behind them, the ten and eleven year old boys walked briskly home from their primary school, eager to prepare for their short boat trip to join their mother and sister. Sione was looking forward to playing cricket with his cousins at Ha'afeva.

He was pleased at the prospect of visiting the island surrounded by pure white sand and where everyone was family. His brother, Tevita, tagged along behind Sione with not a care in the world. Their Dad, Muni, hurried them up. They were soon on their half a mile walk to *Fanga ko Lua-'a-Muni*.

Fig 3. Muni-Mata-Mahae story (torn face): The Hercules of the Pacific.

The trip to Ha'afeva was uneventful. Muni was his usual jovial self, entertaining the passengers. The boys were allowed to dog paddle to the beach while Muni was transferred to a rowing boat for the last leg of the short trip. Uaafe, his wife, had left a few weeks earlier with their youngest child, Mosiana, to see her brother Veikoso and sister 'Ilaise. Uaafe always made gifts of coconut body lotion and tapa cloth for her favourite brother, Veikoso. The boys ran up the beach towards uncle's house.

Panting, Sione immediately sensed that something was very different about the place. Where is Mosiana, their cute little sister? Where is their mum? There were none of the usual smiling faces and welcoming hugs that they had come to expect from their big family here. Through tears, Sione, Tevita and Muni learnt of the unbelievable story of how both mother and daughter had passed away within two weeks of each other.

Mosiana was happily swinging outside under a tree when she fell off and landed awkwardly. She could not be revived. Their mother could not be consoled after the funeral. She fell into a deep depression. Veikoso tried his best to lift her mood but to no avail. Two weeks later, after her brother coaxed her to have a meal he had prepared for her, she obliged, thanked him, then laid down and closed her eyes. She never opened them again.

Veikoso was not able to send a message across to Lofanga about the tragic events. They were very dependent on good weather to cross the waters between the islands of Ha'apai. There were no telephones, no wi-fi connectivity. The pain of losing your little sister and your mum at the same time was too great to bear. On Sunday, at church, their relatives prayed and praised God, asking for his continued blessings on their families and their relatives. Their singing was calming for Sione and gave him some peace.

Back in Lofanga for the New Year celebrations, the residents on the south side of the single road that traverses the island, were preparing the '*umus* (undergound ovens) that year for the communal lunch. Fish, dried octopus, shellfish, roast pigs, yams, taro, tapioca, bananas etc were served up. The residents on the northern side were preparing the communal evening meal of tea, pancakes, dry biscuits and fruits that year. This would alternate the following year.

The next local event was the *Uike Lotu* (week of prayer), when everyone was expected to join in worship at the church each morning and evening of the first week of the year. Routine continued as usual. Soon the boys, Sione and Tevita settled back into their school and daily routine, with their extended families helping the boys whenever required.

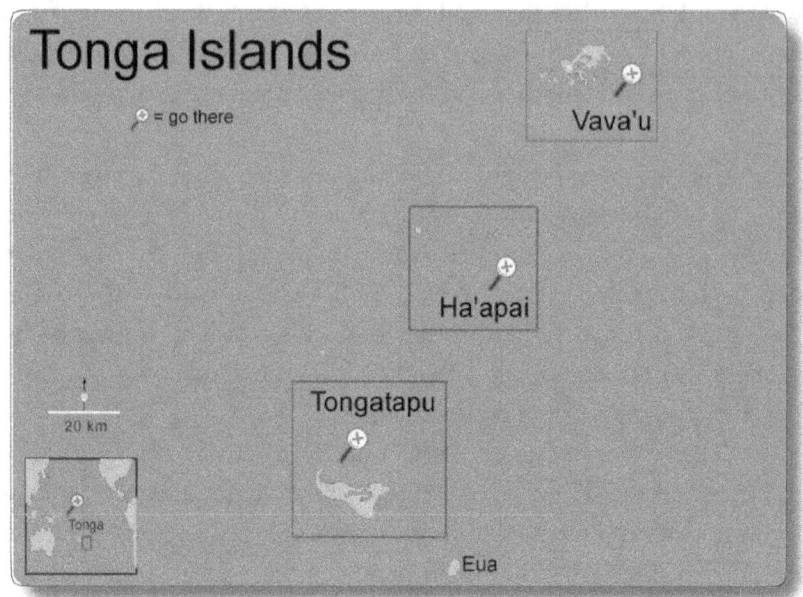

Fig 4. Tonga is comprised of three main groups of islands: Tongatapu in the south, Ha'apai north of Tongatapu, and Vava'u north of Ha'apai. Niuatoputapu and Niua Fo'ou are volcanic islands further north of Vava'u quite close to Fiji.

Siofilisi Tu'ivai, one of Sione's cousins from Lofanga, remembered that many notable students of Tupou College attended Lofanga primary school called Petani. This was most unusual considering the size of this little island and it's small population. From there they sat the entrance exam to Tupou College on the main island of Tongatapu. Sione Finau started at Tupou College, Nafualu, about 1930, at the time of Rev Harold Wood and Dr Olive Wood. Nafualu was a property on the western side of Kolomotu'a. Sia'atoutai Theological College was begun at Nafualu when Tupou College moved to Toloa (it's present site) in 1948.

There are two versions of how the surname of Sione Finau and Tevita, sons of Matapule Muni, became SISIFA instead of MUNI. There were two women in Sione and Tevita's father's upbringing.

According to 'Alekisanita, when he questioned our uncle Tevita (Muni) on the origin of the name Sisifa, our grandfather Viliami MUNI, was adopted by Sisifa, sister of Noble Malupo of 'Uiha. He was often called Viliami Sisifa by the Ha'afeva locals before he was Matapule MUNI. Ha'afeva is the closest island to Lofanga and intermarriage between the two islands was common.

In Pesi's research, the first SISIFA associated with Muni's family was a female who lived in Ha'afeva. Her mother was Siu'ulua, daughter of Noble Malupo of 'Uiha. Her father was Ngalumoetutulu, son of Tu'i Kanokupolu Ma'afu'otu'itonga and a Samoan girl, Ate, from Ha'afeva. This was about 1800. A namesake of this Sisifa in Malupo's family at the time Viliami Muni was born in 1876, continued in Ha'afeva and may have been incorrectly used to register Muni's boys at Tupou College.

The second possible origin of SISIFA was a woman named Mele SISIFA, who lived in Pelehake, an ancient seat of Tongan Royalty. Many of Muni's Lofanga aunties lived in Pelehake. Sione and his brother Tevita, often spent their College weekends and holidays with Muni's relatives in Pelehake. There was a fairly welltodo spinster aunty there called Mele Sisifa, who loved to look after them. A niece of Mele Sisifa, Sela Tafisi, helped with washing their clothes when she was old enough.

When the boys Sione Finau and Tevita entered Tupou College, they gave their surname as Muni. The College Registrar told them that Matapule names cannot be used as surnames (an incorrect statement) and replaced Muni with the name Sisifa instead. That name has stuck with them ever since. (See Appendices)

During their years at Tupou College, the boys, Sione Finau and Tevita, learnt to grow vegetables like *'ufi* (yams), *manioke* (cassava), *kumala* (sweet potatoes), *talo* (taro) and *kape* (arum). They also produced copra from the coconuts. They ate much of their farm products and sold the copra and some vegetables for the maintenance of the school. However, there are records of how hungry the students were during these times. There were two meals a day and they were mainly root vegetables with only leaves cooked in coconut milk to supplement them. No meat was the norm. College boys would longingly be drawn to wafts of delicious food coming from the home of Lu'isa Lakai, wife of the Head Tutor, Rev Sione Havea.

Sione Finau was the Head Prefect of 'Aositelelia House in 1936. He was methodical and meticulous in everything he did, according to Tafolo Lelea of Kolovai. Under his leadership, Sione's school house topped the gardening competition. During the lead up to World War II, Boys Colleges trained the boys in a number of army disciplines. 'Aositelelia House won the artillery drawing competition.

Sione must have enjoyed these gardening experiences. Later in life, Pesi remembers visiting his *'api 'uta* (food gardens) in Kolovai and 'Utulau. She observed her Dad hoeing his garden patches of yams, kumala, or talo. As 'Aleki grew older, Dad thoroughly enjoyed showing him the art of *ngoue* (vegetable gardening) and his knowledge of animal husbandry.

Sione Finau achieved his Maamaloa in 1936. He later achieved his Loumaile as well (the highest achievable award at the time). According to the College records, 1936 saw the highest number of collegians that completed their college courses successfully. 24 boys graduaded from a total of 329 male students. 6 girls graduated out of 119 female students. These excellent results were all the more amazing because 334 students were affected by the onslaught of measles before the exams.

Measles was brought back to Tonga by choir students, sports teams and college representatives who were sent to Australia during this period. (TCSH p249)

Dr 'Amanaki Havea remarked to Lute Aleamotu'a years later, that he believed our Dad's College results would have stood out even more if he had glasses then. He had noticed him straining and rubbing his eyes when reading.

When Pesi was 14 years old in Vaini, she recalled hearing Dad refer to Rev Page when in College. Sione mentioned that he sometimes spent part of his holidays back at the College to help out with the running of the College. He received parcels of books from Dr Wood and Rev Page and other overseas connections from his College years.

During the school years, Sione Finau and Tevita depended on various aunties in Tongatapu to host them and wash their clothes.

Among these aunties were Maikale Taumoepenu in Pea, 'Ana Ma'afu in Kolovai, Mele Sisifa in Pelehake.

SIONE'S CELEBRATORY KAVA AS REMEMBERED BY 82 YEAR OLD TAUMOEPENU ON JUNE 16, 2004

At the end of each year in Tonga, people would converge at their place of birth for Christmas and New Year celebrations. After Sione graduated in 1936, the elders of Lofanga called its people and visitors to gather for a Kava Party and 'Umu to celebrate their son's achievement. Taumoepenu recalls some of the names of close relatives who travelled to be there at the Kava Party: Nehoa (Muni Lahi's brother) and his children 'Ilaisaane and Melepuna; other girls from Tokomololo like Meleseini; Toetu'u and his children and so on. The elder, Toetu'u Tokotaha, in his speech, encouraged all the students and graduates from Lofanga to return to Tongatapu, take on jobs for themselves and help those back in Lofanga. He implored them not to return to Lofanga to paddle canoes and go fishing day in and day out!

Back Row: L-R 'Isikeli Hau'ofa, Kaivai Heimuli, 'Amanaki,.......
Middle Row: L-R 'Ahofitu Maka, Sione Tonga Simiki, Sione Finau Sisifa, Mosese Liongit
Front: L-R Kamipeli Taufa, Lepa Kupu, Howard, Ron, Taniela Fuka, Sinipata 'Uhila

Fig 5. Sione Finau Sisifa at Nafualu 1956.

After this Kava Party, Sione left Lofanga to get his Loumaile and to train as a teacher at Tupou College. He never set foot again in Lofanga. Well known names in Tupou College, government top positions and church leaders whose origin or connections can be traced back to Lofanga and Ha'afeva include Tongilava, Faupula, Molitika, Puniani, Fanua, Tui'ivai, Sisifa (Muni), Veikoso, Simiki and Tukia.

Members of the Tupou College classes of this period who became Tonga's top Government officials, Parliamentarians or Church ministers were: King Taufa'ahau Tupou IV; Governor of Ha'apai Leilua Ve'ehala; Governor of Vava'u, Ma'afu Tupou; Lupeti Finau; Feleti Tupou; 'Uliti Palu; Laufilitonga Tuita; Viliami Tufui; Rev Sione 'Amanaki Havea; Rev Sau Faupula; Rev Viliami Mo'ungaloa; Rev Paula Kongaika. (TCSH)

MAFI ANGAHIKI HELU

Mafi was the youngest child of Sonatane Helu and Taufa Mafile'o of Lotofoa in Foa Island. She was born in 1916 and was surrounded by loving parents, siblings, and extended families on both sides of her parents. This contrasted somewhat with Sione Finau's childhood where his mother came from Ha'afeva and Nuku'alofa and so she with her children, were often absent from Lofanga, to visit her people.

Unlike Lofanga Island, Foa Island is one of a string of islands, and it has 3 villages. Lotofoa is the main village of Foa Island. It is not as isolated as Lofanga. King Tupou 1 resided in Pangai on the Island of Lifuka, for most of his life. Until 2012, people were able to walk to and from Foa Island and Lifuka Island when the tide was out. A causeway was built across the sand/coral strip in 2011 with aid from China. It enabled people to travel across this strip more easily. Cars, trucks and one or two tractors now can travel across from the main town of Pangai to Lotofoa.

Siosaia Fatai Helu, who was Helu IV, on the 21st of October 1938, recorded the history of the origin of the Helu family as follows.

In around 1730, 2 members of the Tu'i Tonga's Falefa (inner circle of 4) consisted of Pahulu and Soakai (Samoan) or Hoakai in Tongan. Pahulu was responsible for accompanying the King around, especially when it was dark, hence the 'hulu' (torch) in his name. When the King required to go somewhere at night, Pahulu would carry a torch made of dried coconut leaves or frond. Soakai was responsible for checking that the food was safe for the King to eat, he would always taste the food before the King had his. According to protocol at the time, only foreigners could perform such tasks, for the King's personal safety reasons.

Pahulu married Soakai's daughter and they had a son called Haveahikule'o. Haveahikule'o made an elaborate headgear or 'helu' for Lekaumoana (Tu'ipelehake 1) when he was on his way to Samoa at one time. Tu'i Lekaumoana, then gave Haveahikule'o the title HELU. Lekaumoana (Pau) is buried in Foa in a Langi called Monotapu.

One of the children of Tu'i Kanokupolu, Mumui (1793), was a daughter called Halaevalu Fonongava'inga. She had 2 children to Haveahikule'o. Her daughter was named Mafikovi Kaunanga and her son was named 'Uhilamoelangi. The line through Mafikovi Kaunanga led to Tungi Mailefihi, as shown on the Helu tree diagram (FT4). Tu'ipelehake of that time, took Haveahikule'o, Helu 1, to Foa, Ha'apai, from Mu'a. When Haveahikule'o, Helu I, died, he was given a burial ground called Houmatala at the Northern end of Lotofoa Island. (Mafi's brother, Hanipale, was buried here in Houmatala. Unfortunately the waves washed away part of this land over some years. In late 2016, his remains were moved by his son, Fatai Helu, and his grandson, Soloni, to the Langi of Tu'ipelehake Lekaumoana in Monotapu, Foa.)

On 16 May 2018, Pesi and her daughter Moana visited the American Museum in Madrid, Spain, to see the second of three Palatavake that Helu 1 made for the Tu'i Tonga, King of Tonga in the 1770s. Both Pesi and Moana felt very emotional and privileged to have had the opportunity to see the intricacies of their great great great great grandfather's handcraft. The head gear had been carefully and delicately restored. Groups of three tu'aniu (midrib of a coconut leaf strand) were tied together with strands of fau. Strips of tapa cloth (painted black with 'koka' paint) bound these triple tu'anius. Three such bound groups were in turn bound together with more black tapa cloth. They were able to observe bits of the ends of the red feathers of the bird Palatavake sticking out through the layers of the groups of tu'aniu posts. The whole headgear would be held up on the wearer's head by a wide band of tapa cloth and strands of kafa (tie made of fibres from coconut husk).

Fig 6. Photo of one of the 3 headgears 'Palatavake'. It was made from the feathers of a rare bird in Tonga called Tavake. It is still being displayed in a Museum in Vienna.

Fig 7. Pesi and Moana admiring the Palatavake displayed at the Madrid American Museum, May 2018.

Fig 8. Close-up photo of the 2nd Palatavake.

Mafi's dad, Sonatane Taufa Helu, was first brought up with the Puloka boys, in Faleloa. They called him Limu (seaweed), because it was his favourite food. He returned to Lotofoa later before marrying Taufa Mafile'o. Taufa Mafile'o was brought up adjacent and behind the Helu compound. Sonatane had a bakery and he was also a builder. He built his family a big weatherboard house and he had a shop beside his house as well as a piggery. His brother, Sioeli Fangatua (Helu III) and his big family lived next door on his left. His sister, 'Ana Mounga, married a German, Frederick Theodore Goedicke and lived next door to Sioeli Fangatua on the other side. Mafi and her siblings were comparatively well to do in Lotofoa. It was known in Mafi's family that their father, Sonatane, helped pay for his brother Sioeli's education as well as Sioeli's children's education.

Around 1918, Mafi's mother Taufa, succumbed to an epidemic of pneumonic influenza introduced by the NZ trading ships. This pandemic wiped out a large proportion of the population in Western Samoa, Fiji and Tonga. Our relatives tell a story about Mafi's dad, Sonatane, sometimes carrying Mafi around to the Kava parties in the evenings when she was about two years old. He would carry a lantern and a portaloo (poo, tapuange mo kimoutolu). About this time, Mafi's father was approached by his nephew Mateaki to marry his defecto wife, Peau Hao'uli, and look after her girls because he really wanted to make Neo Schaaf his wife. Neo was younger, fair skinned and much prettier. Sonatane did as he was bidden and married Peau thus adding two step daughters Siniva and Fualupe to his own big family. When Mafi became a tutor at QSC, she changed their surnames to Helu. This was an act of kindness and inclusiveness that was consistent with how Mafi treated those less fortunate than her. It was not unusual for desirable males to have many children with de facto (df) wives in Tonga at the time.

Sonatane Taufa Helu replaced the original thatched roof of the Weslyan Church (in Lotofoa) with corrugated iron in 1924. This was a very difficult job for a Tongan shaped house. The curves are next to impossible to achieve from corrugated iron. The corrugated iron was placed on level ground and then rolled into shape using a thick pole.

Fig 9. l-r: Sau Malaloi, Hanipale Helu, Vika Fatai Helu outside The Old Church at Foa. Built 1906, dedicated 1913.
Photo 1989 from Fatai F. Helu

Our Grandpa Sonatane fell from a beam during the job. Fortunately, one of his arms became caught in a loop of the 'kafa lalava' (coconut husk rope wound around the beam). Our grandpa was miraculously saved on this day by the rope.

FB article 5th Oct 2017 by Fatai Helu.

Grandpa Sonatane was to die later of another accident to do with this building.

Fualupe, Mafi's stepsister, tells in an interview by Lute and Mele Moala, how Mafi was always so highly organised at home. She always looked very smart in her blue school uniform. She just stood out from all the other girls. Fualupe explained that travelling to Tongatapu from Ha'apai was from Pangai, Lifuka. The boats had no engine so were dependent on good weather and the direction of the winds. It normally took three days, often stopping on route at Felemea and Mango. Most of the time, the Ha'apai students would arrive late for the beginning of term. Other Helu cousins and nieces travelling with Mafi were sister Meliana, niece Susana Helu. Later, step-sisters Siniva and Fualupe Helu, niece Kolotina Helu and niece Lesieli Helu (Lahi) followed. Branches of the Church secondary colleges were commenced at Pangai, Ha'apai in 1946 so these trips were discontinued for the younger students. Fualupe explained how the Helu households were the only ones who had bread and tea for breakfast at the time. This was due to Mafi's father owning his own grocery shop and bakery. Fualupe explained how her mother, Peau, looked after all of them, six of Sonatane's and Peau's two children. Fualupe said that Mafi stayed with Mrs Thompson most of the time when attending QSC, and that cemented her way of life to be like a '*palangi*' (white being from the sky). Mafi mostly kept to herself and her family during her married life. She was not interested in getting herself involved with neighbours to gossip and so on. She devoted her time to making sure her children and husband were fed on time, developed good habits, studied consistently, lived comfortably and observed Christian teachings. Fualupe observed that Mafi was very fond of Dad's dad, Muni. Muni in turn, enjoyed staying with Sione's family and often travelled with them during their ministry.

Fig 10. Neomai Helu Taliai, Siupeli Taliai's mum and Mafi Helu Sisifa's cousin.

Mafi made many lifelong friends from her College days like: Liu Tongilava, Sela Puloka, 'Amelia Kongaika, 'Ungatea Fonua, Latu Mone and 'Etina Havea. Rev A. Harold Wood, the Principal of Tupou College, was big on encouraging social interaction between the boys of Tupou College and the girls of Queen Sālote College. Rev A. H. Wood always had the 'big picture' foresight. He wanted to ensure that the educated boys would marry educated girls to further enhance their future lives. Many of Mafi's school friends married Church ministers. So it was a very successful ploy on Rev A.H. Wood's and Rev Page's part.

Mafi graduated from Queen Sālote College in 1938 with Maamaloa Award. Other Maamaloa recipients that year were: Latai Mo'ungaloa (who married Lupeti Finau), Sela Finau, Mele 'Alofi, Samate, Kaloline Funaki, Kataline Tapani, and 'Amelia Latu. Mafi received her Teacher Certificate at the same time. Her first posting was in Pelehake.

In an interview of Sela Tafisi, when Sela was 79 years old, by Lute and Mele Moala, on 15 June 2004, Sela spoke of Mafi being the first female teacher of the new Pelehake Primary School. Mafi lived in a little Tongan hut. Sela remembered her as a tall, slim, and beautiful looking and gracious young lady. Sela was completely captivated by her. She explained that Mafi always wore puletaha (a frock and a long skirt made of the same material) and a ta'ovala (a short fringed skirt worn as a mark of respect) to work and to church. She was well respected in her town because she was 'highly credentialed' (referring to her Maamaloa Certificate) from QSC. She specialised in teaching Maths and English. She recalled fondly how Mafi taught them to sing the church songs in harmony: Lotu Tauma'u and Temipale Tapu. Mafi often loved to sing soprano in the classroom while beating a little stick on a desk top. After one year, Mafi was recalled to be a tutor at QSC. Sela wistfully remarked, "We lost an exemplary role model from our town."

FT1. Sione Finau Sisifa: Ancestors

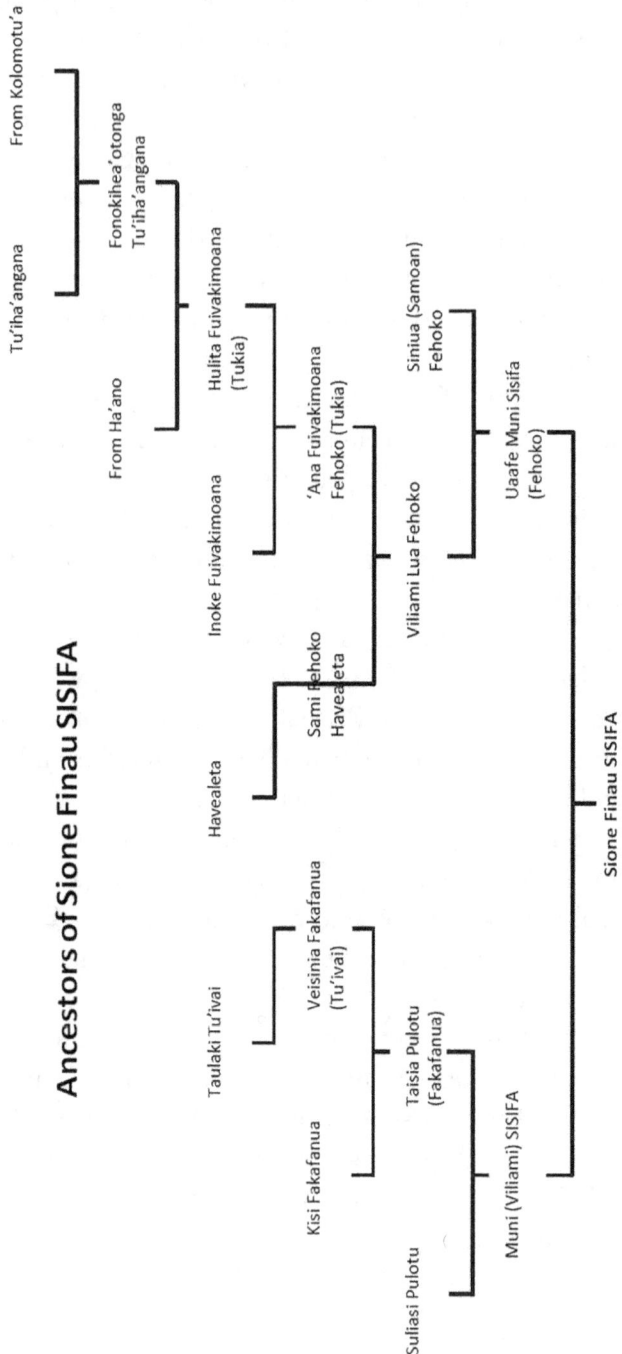

FT2. Mafi Angahiki Helu: Ancestors.

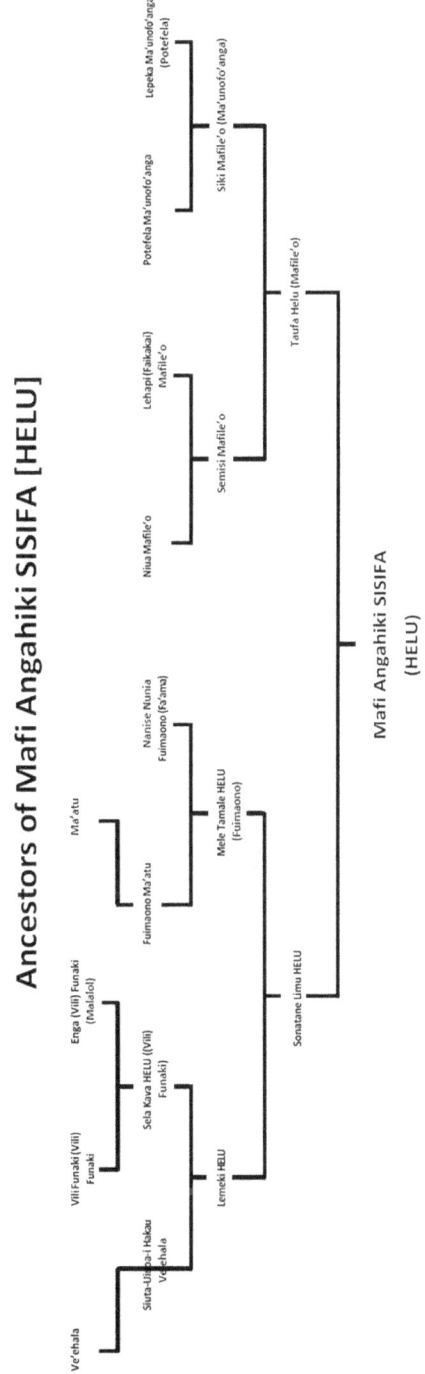

CHAPTER 2

*Don't judge each day by the harvest you
reap but by the seeds you plant.
Robert Louis Stevenson.*

1942-1948 VEITONGO, VAIPOA, FOA TONGA'S INVOLVEMENT WITH WORLD WAR 11

When World War 11 began in Europe in 1938, Tonga was declared at war under its Treaty with the British Government on New Year's Day, 1942. Schools were closed. Only essential services and their workers were allowed to continue working. All European workers in Tonga were evacuated to Fiji and New Zealand. Mrs Mary Thompson, Principal of QSC and Mafi's friend, was a most unwilling evacuee (TCSH p.261). It was during Mrs Thompson's absence in the evacuation that Mafi and Sione Finau got married.

New Zealand handed over defence of Tonga to USA in 1942 and Queen Sālote allowed USA to use Tonga as a base for the duration of the Pacific War. About 12 American warships arrived in April and May 1942. On 9 May, about 7,000 soldiers, 1,000 Navy Personal and a squadron of USA Army Air Corps came on shore. Up to 40 ships were in Nuku'alofa harbour at one stage.

SCHOOL AT VEITONGO

As schools were closed, Sione Finau and his new wife Mafi, were moved to the village of Veitongo straight after they married. There were American soldiers everywhere. Pesi remembers Mafi recalling how scared she was of the black American soldiers. From what Pesi could work out, the black soldiers' behaviour had nothing to do with anything. They were foreigners and she could not see them in the dark!

Many students from schools that Sione and Mafi had taught at, followed Sione and Mafi to Veitongo. For example, Salesi Tupou of Kolovai sent his eldest son Sovea and Fuka sent his son Malolo from Kolomotu'a to Veitongo to attend Sione and Mafi's new school.

An excellent record of their daily routine at Veitongo and especially Mafi's housekeeping skills as a newly wedded young woman, were recorded from an interview of Panitita Helu Piutau (1937 – 2011) on June 2004 by Lute and Mele Moala Aleamotu'a. Panitita Helu was the eldest daughter of Mafi's only brother Hanipale Helu. Hanipale and his wife, 'Akanesi, sent their 5 year old daughter and 4 year old son, Tinitolo to stay with Mafi and Sione Finau.

Panitita Helu Piutau explained that Mafi went to a lot of trouble to make sure her very young charges were distracted from their 'home-sickness'. They were allowed to join school classes if/when they stopped crying! The children were involved in picking little wild tomatoes for their dinner. When the 'big boys' were sent to the beach to collect pipis, crabs and jellyfish for dinner, they were often allowed to join in. Another entertainment activity for them was picking passionfruit from nearby vines.

Meals for the school students and the family included vegetables, taro and pele leaves cooked in coconut milk. Flour and oil were plentiful from the American army supplies. Topai (dough balls made of flour mixed with grated coconut, dropped into boiling water for a few minutes) was often served for breakfast. Mafi used her bread-making skills to bake bread in an underground oven for everyone.

MAFI'S UNDERGROUND OVEN

An underground oven is dug in the ground of the *peito* (cooking outhouse), and half an empty oil drum is lowered into it. The principles of a Tongan *'umu* (or Hangi in Maori) is used. A fire is lit using any burnable sticks, grated coconut shells or wood. About 15 lava stones (not any other type of stone because of likelihood of exploding) are then placed on top of the fire to heat up until red or white hot. Small split sticks of coconut fronds are used to protect the baking tins of uncooked bread from burning.

Baking tins were hand made from sheets of tin. Mafi started a batch of bread dough by fermenting young coconut juice over a few days. Once ready, she would make the bread dough for the first batch. A piece of dough is saved for a few days later to start the next lot of bread making.

According to Panitita, Mafi would bake quite a few loaves as she had many mouths to feed. When the oven was opened up, the aroma of the baked bread was irresistible. Yummy! No wonder they often found locals lined up as well to share Mafi's bread. There was rarely any butter to be had. Mafi improvised by using undiluted cream from the squeezed white scraped coconut flesh. The bread was then dipped into bowls of coconut cream.

Fig 11. Veitongo School, 1943.
Mum and Dad are in the back row, extreme right.
Mum is nursing baby Mosiana in her arms (difficult
to see from the poor quality of the photo).

Modern fads for tea worldwide is herbal tea. At the school in 1942-1943, Mafi improvised with using lemon tree leaves and *moengaloo* (lemongrass) leaves in hot water as their 'tea' to accompany the bread.

Wild tomato plants grew profusely up the school fence. They provided tomatoes that Mafi turned into soup for the mass by adding onions, curry thickened with flour paste. Panitita remembers eating boiled manioke (tapioca) with her tomato soup. The locals caught on to the soup making and 'stole' some of their tomatoes. On reporting this to Mafi, Panitita was persuaded that there was enough for everyone but that they must pick their share early. Panitita remembered being very happy with the food, thinking that they had the best meals in all Veitongo.

Soon, girls joined Sione's and Mafi's school. The girls lived in the big Tongan house with Mafi and the boys stayed in a similar but smaller house with Sione Finau. Every weekend, the students went home, as Sione and Mafi did when they attended College. Under Mafi's guidance, chores like peeling vegetables, cooking the food, cleaning up after meals, and sweeping the grounds were rostered among the students. They worked in pairs, of girl and boy.

Fatai Helu (HELU IV and Futa Helu's dad) was a frequent visitor at Veitongo, so Mafi maintained her close ties with her extended family. Panitita began to notice that Mafi was avoiding carrying heavy bowls, pots, and washing. Mafi must have been pregnant then. Her parents arrived and took their children, Panitita and Tinitolo to Ha'apai, before baby 'Ilaisaane Mosiana was born on 7 March 1943. The name 'Ilaisaane was a Lofanga family name (uncle Nehoa's daughter's name) and Mosiana was Sione Finau's sister's name.

On 4th June 2004 Malolo-'a-Tonga Fuka confirmed to Lute and Mele Moala that he attended Sione's Church primary school in Veitongo during the 2nd World War in 1943. He was 11 years old when Sione and his dad, Fuka, made the decision for him to join Sione's school.

He explained that he enjoyed his life there as it was just like living at home. The atmosphere was relaxed and pleasant with no strict rules. In the classroom, both Mafi and Sione had a well-balanced program, and they were considerate, and kind. He said, "We students loved it there, none of us was homesick." Mosiana was born during this time, and Malolo said he babysat her often.

SIONE FINAU SISIFA'S ORDINATION AS A METHODIST MINISTER

Sione Finau had been a candidate for the Methodist Ministry, while he was teaching from 1940 to 1944. He was ordained as a Church Minister in June 1944. As Mafi was 6 months pregnant at the time with their second child, Sione Finau left for their first posting at Vaipoa, Niuatoputapu, without Mafi and Mosiana. However, he was not on his own, as his dad Muni, accompanied him. Mafi, with Mosiana, moved to Tokomololo to stay with her aunts (sisters of her mum's, Toakase and 'Ana Hosea) until her second child was born. Mafi's brother and his wife, Hanipale and 'Akanesi, were over from Lotofoa during this time. 'Elenoa Lute was born on 15 September 1944. The name Lute (Ruth) was chosen from the Bible, 'Elenoa was Sione and Mafi's own choice.

SIONE'S FIRST POSTING AS A CHURCH MINISTER, VAIPOA

Niuatoputapu (Sacred Niua), is one of the furtherest islands north of Tongatapu. Apparently, this distant posting was to facilitate the fact that when the children grew older, church ministers needed to be nearer the Colleges in Tongatapu. Niuatoputapu is nearer Samoa and Fiji than it is to Tongatapu, (that is why it could not be included in the Map of Tongatapu (fig 3). It is a high island as it is volcanic in origin. Vaipoa is the middle village in the island and second in size to the capital of Niuatoputapu, Hihifo (meaning west).

To the immediate south of Vaipoa is the crumbling remains of the centre of the volcano. To the north east of the beach village, Vaipoa, is the imposing island of Tafahi (strike and split). Tafahi is about 9 km by boat from Vaipoa. There is a deep and often rough channel between the two islands. Tafahi was under Sione's ministerial responsibility. His account of his trip there is testament to his romantic and poetic leaning. (In Tongan: p233.)

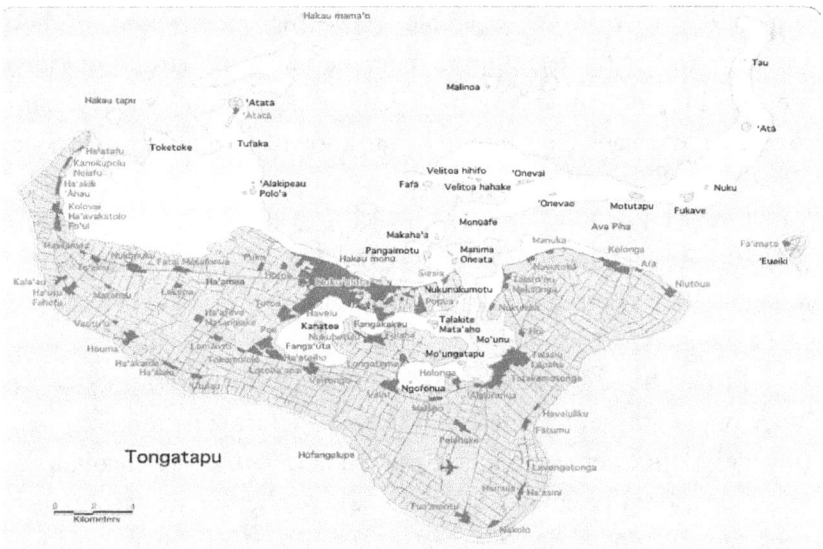

Fig 12. A map of Tongatapu.

KOE KI'I KOLO KAKALA 'O FUNGA FAONO (THE FRAGRANT VILLAGE ON TOP FORTYSIX)

There is already a 'Fragrant Town' in Tongatapu: Mu'a. That town is one of the most important Seats of Royal families. Sione prefaced his report by apologising for using this term to rename the small township on the island of Tafahi.

Sione estimated the height of the village is 50 feet above sea level and the volcano itself to be half as high as Tofua in the Ha'apai Group. (In fact, the highest point of the volcano itself is 610m while that of Tofua is 1,030m.) This island was already populated before the two papalangi, Schouten and Lemaire (Dutch voyagers) visited the Niuas in 1616. There were at least 20 adults at the time of Sione's visit. He estimated the town was of the size of 'Utulau then.

He thought everyone looked healthy. He was amazed at how edible plants sprouted up in every nook and cranny amongst the volcanic rocks. They grew fast and produced abundant fruits non-stop. Coming from a vegetable gardening background in both Lofanga and at College, Sione marvelled at this 'Garden of Eden'. The local Chief named Mosese Vaka, had been wanting a new name for his little village. Up till then it was known as Tafahi as well. Sione Finau and Mosese Vaka renamed the village as KOLO KAKALA 'O FUNGA FAONO or for short, KOLO KAKALA 'O FUNGA (FRAGRANT VILLAGE ON TOP). Faono refers to the year of renaming (1946) to distinquish this village to that of the town of Mu'a, Tongatapu.

Just as the edible fruits were abundant, so were perfumed plants. They popped up everywhere and grew very fast. The tangled 'maile' (myrtle) plants were so fragrant that they were used in coconut skin oil production. The small pale land snails, *pueki*, that are used to make necklaces, handbags, decorate mats and *ta'ovala* (waistmats) are found only here at Tafahi. That is why pueki is a rare commodity and hence valuable in Tonga.

There were no horses in Tafahi. The contour of the land is very rocky and rough. Hence it was not easy for the men to reach their allotments (8 acre government designated plot of land or *'api'uta*), nor to cart home their wood for fire, coconuts, yams, manioke etc. Each home had a man-made horse. It consisted of 2 poles tied together and worn around the neck. When loaded with the products from their 'api'uta, the horse is carried horizontally on the shoulders of 2 people (normally a man and his wife or son).

Sione concluded his report by asking those in the *Akolotu* (every youth in his flock) to strive to grow the seeds of Love, Faith, Hope, Forgiveness, Kindness and Peace, so they can develop and bloom into useful 'fragrant' citizens. They would make everyone proud: God and the Church, their family, their town and the Kingdom of Tonga. He prayed that each member would mature into a desirable "fragrant" person in character. God loves to dwell in such "fragrant towns".

> As Hymn 510 reads:
>
> Loto moe 'atamai
> Ko ho pule'anga ia
> Fotu'u taloni ai
> Tala ai ho fatongia.
> Take my will, and make it thine;
> It shall be no longer mine.
> Take my heart it is Thine own;
> It shall be Thy royal throne.

Sione signed off with:

> *"In expectation of fragrant rewards to
> clothe you in the Heavenly Realms."*

Siupeli Taliai, in his book *'E keu 'elelo afe mai*, page 178, explained that the author of this hymn, Frances Ridley Havergal, in the previous verses had dedicated her wealth, her voice, her lips, her children, her dwelling, her hands, her brilliant mind, her power, to God. In this verse, Frances says they are not enough, she is also dedicating her will and her heart. In other words, all our talents should be dedicated to God alone to use as He pleases. Siupeli further explains that this does not mean to literally donate all our earnings to worthy courses and ignore our earthly needs. Frances was referring to her offering of all her talents to please God and never to do anything evil with them.

Fig 13. Tafahi as seen from a Niuatoputapu beach

This picture of Tavi and his lean-to are included here as he had become a sort of folklore figure in Tafahi and other isolated parts of Tonga. Tavi was a Norwegian engineer who found his way to Tonga. He arrived in Tonga in 1950 in search of somewhere warmer and which would give him 'more reason to live.' His huge knowledge on Tongan society was from Havea Tu'i Ha'ateiho of the time. Tavi assisted Elizabeth Bott to document Captain Cook's diary of his visits to Tonga in Memoir No. 44 and also relied heavily on the extensive knowledge of Her Majesty Queen Sālote. Thomas Riddle documented his amazing friendship with Tavi at www.thomasriddle.net/tavi website and in his book on Tavi.

Fig 14. Tavi and his abode (opposite) in Tafahi,
apparently built between 2 boulders
www.thomasriddle.net/tavi/index.html

Pesi considers that the 'only' other important family occurrence at this posting, as far as she is concerned, was her birth. (Her siblings are hotly disputing this!) Nevertheless, 'Ilisapesi Lina Sisifa was born in the morning of 15 March 1946. In those days, the Tongan Government produced and distributed large wall calendars. That year, the calendar had a photo of Queen Elizabeth, in her full regalia, on the top of the 1946 calendar. Such a calendar adorned my parents' room wall. They bestowed the Queen of England's names, Elizabeth Regina on their third daughter. Regina was simplified to Lina. The Tongan language does not have the letter R, so it's normally replaced by L. G is used in conjuction with the letter N in front of it (ng) to produce a different sound to that of the English G.

LOTOFOA IN HA'APAI AND HIHIFO IN NIUATOTAPU

'Alekisanita wrote in September 2004 (at our first sibling-get-together in Suva, Fiji).

From Whence I Came

Of humble beginnings I came into this world in the early hours of the morning of 4th January 1948 after the Second World War, at Lotofoa, Ha'apai. I had always thought the sun virtually shone through my mother, Mafi. She was love exemplified to me and all around her. My father, Sione, was the model of the good Tongan i.e. a Minister of the Weslyan Church. I know he tried very hard to share as much of his busy time as he could with me. That I appreciate very much.

Mafi, herself being from Lotofoa, and I, as the firstborn son of Sione, meant I was accorded a name thought appropriate by her family. Actually, as the first son of Sione, I would have thought Viliami (Muni) would have stood his ground and provided my name. But then 'Sione' and 'Tevita' as generic names for his own sons were not innovative. The fact the sons themselves nor Viliami Muni did not insist during registration procedures on entrance to Tupou College to keep their surname as their Title name, as practised by many titled families, does perhaps say something about the nature of my grandfather.

As it was, my name *'Alekisanita* was given by who else but Mafi's aunt, 'Ana Mo'unga Goedicke ('Ana Feleti Kaa). 'Ana Mo'unga was married to Frederick Theodore Goedicke. Fred or Feleti Kaa, was a business man/trader in Tongatapu and Ha'apai at the time. 'Ana Feleti and Feleti Kaa's eldest son was named Alexander. Frederick Goedicke was originally from Germany and was the son of Thomas Goedicke (mayor and chemist) and Ida Schluter. Ida Schluter's father was Consul for Hanover and her mother was from a wealthy textile industrialist/Countess family.

Uinoa-i-Hakau was the name of Mafi's great grandfather, who was a son of Noble Ve'ehala, FT 2. Preceeding my birth, the Weslyan Church band of Lotofoa was fundraising to buy brass band instruments. The aim was £10,000. If successful, my third name would have been *Mano* (ten thousand). As it turned out, I had to be contented with *Fiemano* (in need of ten thousand) as part of my name.

'Ana and Fred Goedicke had 2 sons, named Alexander Goedicke and Theodore Goedicke. Theodore died aged 1. Alexander went to Auckland for his education. He married Hilda Clark. They had a daughter, Phyllis Goedicke who married Owen Beer in 1971. They lived in Avondale, Auckland. Alexander died in 1966. (From Geneologist Kit Withers, c.withers@irl.cri.nz)

The first Brass Band in Tonga was the Police Band. Lotofoa had the second, in 1948. Only one instrument remains of this first lot. The rest were replaced in the 1980s.

Source: Fatai Helu's FB article 5th Oct 2017.
Fatai is the second youngest son of
Hanipale Helu (Mafi's only brother).

'Aleki continued:

Sione's father, Muni (Viliami) was with our family in Lotofoa when, I was born. Muni died just after I was born. I learnt from Mafi's sisters Numia, 'Ana, Meliana and brother Hanipale, that I used to play on top of Muni's tomb.

Apparently, when I was born, Lotofoa was virtually busting at the seams. Lotofoa was a large village by Tongan standards and all town allotments had houses (thatched, weatherboard or brick) built there. Helu and Malaloi as Matapule names were well known and holders were known for having robust fortunes in terms of crops and livestock ownership. I visited Lotofoa a number of times in connection with my job in Government. In the late 1970s the town was still well occupied and prosperous. But by the early 1990s, there were conspicuous signs of dereliction. Absentee landowners was becoming very common. (Matapule Malaloi came from another branch of the Helu family, Sionatane Siale.)

Lute's and Pesi's recollections of Lotofoa.

Mosiana and Lute started school in Foa at the Church Primary School next door to the family home on its left. Lute remembers learning to write on a small blackboard slab using chalk until about class 3. She was punished (hit on her left hand with a ruler) to make her use her right hand for writing. There are many left-handers in our family now but that was viewed as a handicap in education then!

We lived in a big weatherboard house with lots of mango trees on its right-hand side. The Helu 'api kolo' (family compound) was on the left side (north) of the primary school. This made it easy for Mafi and her children to visit their relatives, both her dad's (Sonatane Helu) and her mum's (Taufa Mafile'o) and brother 'Uiha.

Pesi used to dream for years of anticipating checking out for ripe juicy mangoes that may have dropped on the ground overnight. She recalls also the bent-over figure of great aunt 'Ana Feleti Kaa. She was a never ending source of sweet biscuits. She had grey hair and always appeared busy. What Pesi can't remember, Mosiana reminds her. For example, running away from mum, turning up at school before mum had put her clothes on. These are best forgotten incidences as far as Pesi is concerned.

Pesi can remember grandfather Muni's antics. Vaipoa people remembered him for his jokes. He played tricks with his grandchildren in Foa. One such trick was to line up his three little granddaughters, use his fore fingers and thumbs to form two circles, then look through them while pretending to strain his eyes to find the most beautiful granddaughter. To Pesi's delight and absolute despair of her older sisters, she was always declared the prettiest!

Sadly, Pesi also remembers the day when grandfather, Viliami Muni had his fatal stroke. At his ripe old age of 72, he had a stroke on his way home from the vegetable garden near the reef. It was nearing evening meal time. The rest of the family were milling around when there was a big kerfuffle with grandfather being carried into the lounge. Grandfather seemed to recover somewhat. However, during that night, he passed away. People arrived from everywhere. Our house remained full of people for many days afterwards.

I best remember my grandfather Muni as a kind, happy and hardworking person.

Fig 15. The beach at Lotofoa beyond all the town's vegetable gardens.

*Happiness resides not in possessions, not
in gold, Happiness dwells in the soul.
Democritus*

Fig 16. Evening at Faleloa on Foa Island.

Fig 17. Fresh food in Lotofoa:
lobsters; baskets of yams, pawpaw and taro leaves; fish.

CHAPTER 3

*Even if I knew that tomorrow the world will go
to pieces, I would still plant my apple tree.*
Martin Luther

NIUATOPUTAPU 1950-1952

'Aleki wrote on Niuatoputapu

I was 2 years old when we landed in Hihifo, Niuatoputapu, for the first time for me (second for the rest of the family). When we left for Tongatapu, I was 5 years old. Memories are hazy fifty years after leaving this island.

I remember a few people and a few events, some of both probably from second and third hand accounts from my parents.

A Lofanga boat builder, Vili Suli lived not too far from our home I think he went there to help our family. His son, who was the same age as me, had a white dog. I had a rooster (red in colour) that was the envy of young boys at the time because it beat all other roosters at cockfights in the neighbourhood. I took a liking to the white dog and tried to persuade Vili Suli's son, 'Esala, for an exchange – the dog for the rooster. He was not willing at all. I asked my father to negotiate at his level. There is something about being a Church minister in an island like Niua. Vili Suli convinced his son and the exchange was made. Lute explained that 'Esala's sister Loueni, informed her that 'Esala is in Lofanga now (2004) looking after our inherited tax allotment ('api 'uta, which is three times the size of everyone else's 'api 'uta) and our town allotment, 'api kolo.

By inheritance, this is Sione's land, as the eldest in his family and followed by 'Alekisanita, Sione's eldest son. All titled families in

Tonga, nobles (nopele) and spokespersons (matapule) must perform designated duties to the King or Queen, especially if they visit your town or island (tofi'a) or when summoned to the palace for certain duties.

The story about "Nita" protecting our school luncheons was classic. During our last year in Niua, at 4 years old, I tagged along to school with the girls. Mafi would have prepared our lunches and secured them within one good sized billy in a cotton bag, which one of the girls would carry. Normally, we would stroll for a small distance then side track to the sandy beach and only leaving the sand when reaching the school. One day, we stopped on the beach for a while because the girls were playing and we left without the lunch bag. It was not until morning break that the girls found the lunch bag missing. The girls traced their way back onto the beach in search of the lunches. Nita was sitting on guard where the bag was. What made this story profound was the fact that a fisherman who was in the area at the time, told our father during a Sunday kava party, that he saw the bag where he was casting his net but when he approached to investigate, Nita would growl and barked so hard he had to retreat and finally leave.

I named him "Nita", short version of 'Alekisanita and apparently he was quite intelligent. Still imprinted in my mind is Nita swimming after the MV Hifofua with us on board when we left for Tongatapu a kind youth had to get into the water to retrieve him.

Mosiana, Lute and Pesi all remember 'Aleki's dog fondly. Lute added that Lopeti Taufa years later, used this story of Nita at Saione (the 'Methodist main Church' in Nuku'alofa) as an example of faithfulness. Lopeti Taufa then told Lute that he actually took Nita home and adopted him as Nita would not stay where we lived. Lopeti Taufa taught us at Vaipoa during our dad's posting at Hihifo. He now is a retired President of the Methodist Church of Tonga and lives with his family in Nuku'alofa. Lopeti married one of our Simiki (Smith) cousins, Mele.

'Aleki continued:

The boat trip from Niuatoputapu to Tongatapu was something that whilst not too clear in my mind, I could recall certain aspects and feelings when I was on the more recent version of the boat MV Hifofua (sails and inboard motor) going from Nuku'alofa through Pangai to Neiafu on an agricultural show trip in the late 1970s, accompanying Tomasi Simiki and the Royal party.

A gentleman named Malekamu Manu was the Postmaster at the time in NTT. He had a number of boys older than me and whom I got to know well later in life. His daughter, 'Ainise, and I got to be in the same class about 7 years later in Tonga High School. She was my age and she used to join me and my friends in games of mock *'Umu'*, *lanitaa*, and cricket. Our 'cricket' used the midrib of a coconut frond for a bat, oranges or grapefruits for balls. We made carts using the grapefruits shaped with knives for the wheels.

A medical doctor named 'Opeti Lutui, was working in Niuatoputapu at the time. I later got to know him well in the 1970s and 80s when I returned from Australia to work in Tonga. He was then a very senior medical officer/superintendent. Dr 'O. Lutui must have presided over the delivery of my sister Mele Teufolau Sisifa in the morning of 30 May 1952. Dr Lutui passed away at the end of the 20th century.

In Niua, I remember Dr Lutui particularly for his dove shooting escapades. He would return with a bag half full of doves, and he would give Mafi two or three of these birds. The dove fat (especially around the gut and heart/lung areas) is really something of a delicacy – darkish yellow with an extremely attractive odour and taste. I used to love dipping yam, taro or cassava into this fat and then eating it.

> *Pesi recalls how years after, she romantisized about this big gentleman riding into our home with a gun attached to the side of the horse, a brimmed hat and a bag full of birds. That is how she imagined Mr Darcy when reading*

Jane Austen's novel, Pride and Prejudice at Epsom Girls Grammar at Auckland in 1962.

Talking about food, there are a number of gathering activities that are imprinted in my mind. The 'Lailo' or mud crabs, when the season was on, 6-7 men and women including Dad, would go after them and would come back in the early hours with the large catches. Lailo cooked in thick coconut milk was delicious.

There are two community fishing methods that I remember from my time in Niuatoputapu (NTT) and reinforced with information gathered later in life. One is called 'Aukava', using the organic compound in a 'kavakava ulie' product of pepper or capsicum family to poison the fish. The community would collect all and divide the spoils among themselves. Before the event, people would go to the bush to collect the kavakava ulie, stock them up then gather at the reefs just before low tide and pound the plant roots on the rocks near the reefs. When the tide is at its lowest, the fish would then be seen floating across the reefs.

The other community fishing method was the Ūloa, one that I think was very environmentally friendly. Unlike *'Aukava*, it did not indiscriminantly kill sea life. Mounting a Ūloa took a lot of preparatory work. A great quantity of coconut fronds have to be cut down from the palms, split along the midrib and tied lengthwise (or in later times into thin ropes). For a Ūloa, I now estimate there would need to be at least 4000 ft of these long strands of coconut fronds-ropes. The Ūloa would start when the tide conditions are receding from high to low, closer to low than to high. On the day of the Ūloa and when the conditions are right, the village population (including oldies and youngies) of men and women, would hold the strands at predetermined intervals. They would advance towards the beach from the reefs, lifting and lowering the strands at the same time, shouting and beating the sea with whatever means (hands, knives, sticks) and generally making a pandemonium. In so doing the fish would be driven in and concentrated close to the beach, where everyone would then catch and kill them with spears, knives and with their bare hands. I think customarily, families would take their catches home but then some would be given supplements if they were not too successful.

Fig 18. Preparing for the Ūloa in Niuatoputapu, with the base of Tafahi visible in the background.
(*Source: Ethnobiology of Coral Reefs.*)

Catches from the above community based activities and from individualistic efforts using nets, and line and hook, were often more than could be eaten within one or two meal times. There were two ways of overcoming this problem. One was to distribute to neighbours and getting reciprocal favours when they had their own successes. The other was to prepare a good sized *'Umu*, weave fresh *si* leaves or banana leaves around the fish and bake them. Then the baked fish would be stored in coconut frond baskets hung from the rafters of the kitchen. Such fish, if well cooked and dry, would remain in good condition for a week or so. There were some innovative ways of improving the palatability of food in island life. In NTT, the use of *'hami'* is of particular interest. That is because the smell is revulsion personified. A green coconut having about 0.25 inch thick meat is opened on one end then little chilli and bits of coconut meat are left inside. The open coconut then is filled with sea water, the small lid replaced and the whole concoction is hung from the rafter of the kitchen to cure. It is ready to consume after a week or so. The smell is terrible, the taste even worst. (Pesi likens it to some of the most pungent cheeses in Europe.) In combination with a bit of pig fat and salt or as sole accompaniment for yam, taro, banana, cassava etc, the hami can encourage the eater to a bigger intake compared to without it.

I later visited the Niuas (NTT and Niua Fo'ou) and Ha'apai in the 1980s. I visited NTT five times. I was to learn during these visits how people value their relationships with the Church ministers. Many of the men I met over these visits, related to me fond memories of Sione and Mafi over kava.

Lute and Pesi remember

Mosiana was 6 years old, Lute 5 and Pesi 3 years old when we arrived at Hihifo, NTT. We girls also remember Hihifo fondly as a dream place to grow up in. Lute salivates at the thought of the row of tava trees on the northern boundary of our compound. On the eastern boundary were breadfruit trees. A big enclosed tin shed was in the far corner of the block, facing the church in the south. Our big weatherboard house faced the west, which overlooked a big field, and led to the infamous spring water river that we older children loved so much. Paula Vivili's family lived beside the river, and overlooked the sea towards the beautiful island of Hunganga.

Lute had a fear of darkness. One evening, she took a lamp with her to visit the children's toilet (*tapuange mo kimoutolu*). Dad had a small sized one made for us children. Sitting there in the dark, Lute closed her eyes tightly to prevent seeing any monsters. Bedtime approached, no Lute. Our parents raced around searching for her. To their absolute relief, Dad saw the lamp and found Lute fast asleep at the toilet.

Another expatriate from Nuku'alofa was Magistrate Hingano Helu. He was Fatai Helu IV's son and our mum's nephew. Hingano and his wife, Mafi, had a daughter named 'Eseta. 'Eseta was a bit older than Mosiana. Adding to the four of us Sisifa children, were playmates 'Ainise Manu, and her brother Viliami. We were never lacking games to play. Our most enjoyable activity was swimming at the Spring water river mentioned before which was half a kilometre from home. Unfortunately, Malekamu's children and 'Aleki were too little to come swimming with us. Games included hide and seek inside and outside our house, hopscotch, cards, riding our dad's bicycle, skipping and playing marbles. The girls often made leis of frangipani and dandelion chains. We made kites from sheets of paper and *tu'aniu* (the coconut leaves' midrib). The kite tail was made from old tapa cloths (torn from the edge of one of the children's tapa cloth bedding without our mum's knowledge). We used normal sewing cotton so the whole kite had to be quite light to be able to fly.

Lute remembers trying to collect mature coconuts from the church *'api 'uta* to help Dad. The ground, being very fertile and moist, seemed to always be covered with red millipedes. We, children, dreaded stepping on them. At home, dad would split the coconuts. He and mum would sit with knives and *hihi niu* (scrape out the white flesh from the coconut shells). The children would help carry the white coconut meat to our *fale ta'oniu* (copra drying shed) which Dad had built beside the out kitchen/dining hut. The coconut husks then would be ferried to where they could easily be fed into the furnace in the drying shed. The furnace was made of kerosene drums that were opened on both ends and laid end to end. (This is the same kerosene drum that Mafi's underground oven was made from.)

All kitchens in Tonga at the time were out kitchens. It was necessary as cooking was over open fires. Most homes also ate their meals in the out kitchens. We had a dining room or separate dining outhouse in most 'api faifekau we lived in.

Fig 19. (Above & next page) Two views of Vai ko Niutoua, Niuatoputapu Island, Tonga. 6 May 2010.

When the coconut slices were dried (now called copra), they were placed into hessian bags. The MV Hifofua arrived with the grocery and medical supplies for Niuatoputapu about every 6 months. Paula Lava from the Copra Board came to weigh the copra bags and gave us cash in return. Dad would bank some of the takings and use the rest to send an order to the Church Office in Nuku'alofa for our home supplies to be sent in the next boat to NTT.

The family supply orders included items like bags of flour and sugar, boxes of corned beef, tinned herrings, kerosene tins for our kerosene lamps, benzene for the gas lamp, cigarettes for dad, jars of jam, large tins of maa pakupaku (dried biscuits), tinned butter etc. Opposite Vivili's house and beside the river was the main shop of Hihifo. It was owned by the Gustuv family. When boats were held up due to bad weather and the shops would run out of their goods, the Government officers came to our house to ask for a share from our supply shed.

There were plenteous cotton tree plants and the cotton wool balls that were blown around everywhere. These cotton balls, when harvested, were sold or used for mattresses and pillows and distributed throughout Tonga. Lime plants grew profusely here in Niuatoputapu. Mum used the lime for cooking and bottling lime juice drinks and the lime fruits were also sent to the rest of Tonga.

Later in life we met up with many of the neighbours from Hihifo and their children in Colleges or overseas.

Fig 20. The map of Niuatoputapu

Solo Taufe'ulungaki was a Government primary school principal. We were friends with his daughters. Lupe and Pisila were excellent students at Queen Sālote College and they studied overseas at University level. 'Ana, who is may be of 'Aleki's age, studied at Tonga High School (THS), Epsom Girls Grammar School and Auckland Unversity. She has a Ph. D and was the previous Director of Education and later the Minister of Education, Women's Affairs and Culture (despite not being a Politician).

Mum had a nephew and niece living in Hihifo. Mum's first cousin, Dr Kuli Helu, worked in Hihifo a few years before our posting there. He had a de facto partner there and two children named 'Ana Mo'unga and Holaki Helu (named after Dr Kuli Helu's youngest brother who died very young). Mafi often took us around to see these children and their mother.

Another neighbour was the Fakasi'ieiki or Motu'ahala family. Motu'ahala is a matapule assisting Ma'atu, the noble of Niuatoputapu. At church Ma'atu's family sat at the front of the church and to the left of the pulpit. The minister's family sat on the right. These areas were fenced off from the rest of the congregation. One of Hanipale's granddaughters, 'Akanesi, is married to a grandson of the Fakasi'i'eiki family named Kanongata'a and they live in Melbourne, Australia.

There is Helu family link to Fuimaono in NTT. Lemeki Helu (Helu III), Mafi's grandfather, married Mele Tamale Fuimaono. Mele Fuimaono's mother was a Samoan named Nanise Numia from a Western Samoan island called Manono, in the village of Lefanga. Her father, Fuimaono, was the youngest son of Ma'atu, Noble of NTT. Lute remembers Fuimaono's son, 'Ukakala, often arriving on a bicycle with cooked food from Uncle Fuimaono, to his niece Mafi. Here in Melbourne, we have met up with some Fuimaono descendents!

Fig 21. This is a much bigger and more modern version of the MV Hifofua that Rev Sisifa and his family sailed on in the early 1950s to and from Niuatoputapu. (From *Tongan Story*)

Fuimaono (of late eighteeth century) had a sister, called Fehi'a who was the second wife of 'Ulukalala-'i-Ma'ufanga. Their son's name was Tupouniua. 'Ulukalala-'i-Ma'ofanga was also the father of the notorious Finau 'Ulukalala who attacked the Port au Prince and murdered all on board except Mariner.

It was traditional on Sundays that lunch was preceded by food exchange with the neighbours. There was always a siesta on Sunday before all children got dressed again to attend Sunday school. This was conducted by volunteers from the church community. At these sessions, all children got to learn Biblical stories like those of Abraham, Moses and the Exodus; they recited Psalms, learnt to act out the stories. There was a lot of learning by rote. Every year on the first Sunday of May, there is a children's festival called Fakamee. The Sunday School children recite the verses of the Hymns and the Readings of the morning service. Every child is dressed in their new clothes and lunch consists of extra special foods. In the afternoon, the church gathers again for the children to act out the Biblical stories.

Choir practices in the Hihifo Church at night were particularly memorable. Choirs from many churches were to compete in Nuku'alofa when the new Methodist Centenary Building (Saione) was to be consecrated. The Sisifa family were sung to sleep by the triumphant refrain of F.Handel's 'Halleluia Chorus' for months on end. Malekamu Manu, the postmaster, was the choir master and conductor.

Pesi remembers how enjoyable primary school was. She had picked up reading and the times tables from Mosiana and Lute.

Every weekday after dinner, our gas lamp would be shifted from the kitchen to the lounge where evening learning was to take place. The times tables were recited and the three girls would compete as to who could recite each table the fastest. Mosiana and Lute were dismayed if Pesi beat them. These homework sessions gave Pesi an excellent basis for her career in Mathematics. Throughout her student years, her numerical calculations were visually aided by the playing of card games at this time. Lopeti Taufa, the Primary School teacher at

Vaipoa Primary School announced to Dad that Pesi would skip one class.

CHURCH MINISTRY

As the children grew up, the most influential social force in their young lives was of course the Methodist Church activities. Every Saturday, the children would be sweeping the leaves outside. Mounds of these leaves and branches would be burnt. There was no such thing as carbon footprints then! The smoke produced by all the homes burning off their rubbish was part and parcel of the cleaning up your home in preparation for Sunday. The church congregation, at every quarter would draw up a roster of offers to host the Sunday preachers. This could be in the form of a family feast to mark a special family event of the host, or, the host would provide uncooked food in a big basket made from fresh coconut fronds, to deliver on Saturday evening to the home of the preacher. As Dad almost always preached on Sunday in the town we lived in or a village in his district, we had no shortage of food for Sunday.

Sunday was a special and sacred day. It started with Mum preparing the *'umu* in her underground oven. She would also serve light breakfast of homemade bread and tea. All the children would dress in their Sunday best. In the meantime, our lounge would start to fill up with other dads and granddads who came for a kava party before church. Dad would preside over these kava parties. Later in life, the children enjoyed eavesdropping from their bedrooms on these talk-fests in the lounge. This was a chance for fathers to voice their opinions on the past week's events and maybe boast about their children's achievements. Apparently, Dad rebuked his own dad once or twice for boasting about his son Sione's achievements! A young woman from the church community always came to prepare the kava drink. At about 9am on Sunday, all church bells and *lali* (wooden drums) let loose a cacophony of sounds everywhere in the islands that made up the country of Tonga, calling everyone to church.

Mele Moala Aleamotu'a found the following report Sione Finau had written for the *Church Quarterly News* 1953 from Niuatoputapu.

> *We hereby wish to thank Her Majesty, Queen Sālote Tupou, for her support in enabling women leaders of the Church from Tongatapu to travel to Niuatoputapu to hold a Conference for the Kaluseti Group. We were very excited to welcome he 5-member group on 6th May 1953: Kalolaine Lavaka, 'Alisi Hama, 'Ana Seini, Tupou Kafa and 'Ahofa Talakai. A welcoming evening event was organised and chaired by Rev Sione Sisifa. 'Alisi Hama explained the focus of the Women's Kaluseti Group. 'Ana Seini spoke on the aims of the 'Conference', and Kalolaine Lavaka spoke on 'The Good Samaritan'. The evening concluded with Maletina Tupou (Minister's wife from Vaipoa) and Mafi Sisifa thanking the visitors. In the next 2 days, many sessions were conducted to explain and discuss passages from the Bible and how to follow in Christ's footsteps.*

Tangimana lived in Hihifo, Niuatoputapu, when Sione and Mafi worked there in 1950 to 1952. He was living in Kolomotu'a when Lute and Mele Moala Aleamotu'a caught up with him for an interview on 20 June 2004.

Tangimana recalled many housekeeping stories as he was a young man who enjoyed helping Dad. He remembered the family breakfasts of bread or pancakes. He talked about Dad making copra from 2 'api 'utas belonging to the church. He remembered Dad's copra drying shed which Dad left to him after our family moved back to Tongatapu.

He recounted how Mum and Dad had so much of everything due to their hard work. He grew a lot of yams and other vegetables, keeping pigs, chickens, as well as going fishing. Then people would bring their, *polopolo* (first fruits), or their best yield of bananas, hopa, 'ufi etc. Tangimana also knew about Rev Sione's shed that had so many different types of goods for when the goods boats did not turn up on time. He noted that Mum and Dad were very sparing and never wasteful, in the way they lived.

One anecdote was about a visiting palangi faifekau, Rev Grove, Chairman of Vava'u and Ha'apai Districts. On the Sunday morning, Dad asked Tangimana to take Kolove (Rev Grove) on a cart to preach at Vaipoa, then Falehau and finally back at Hihifo in the evening. Dad told Tangimana to listen carefully to Rev Grove's services as he expected him to learn them off by heart. Tangimana laughed when he found out what Dad meant. Reverend Grove repeated his sermon 3 times that day, word for word! Rev Grove asked for some cigarettes before they left in the morning. Dad gave him a whole packet. Tangimana was astounded at how Rev Grove had a cigarette in his mouth all the way to Falehau and back. When they pulled up at Hihifo, he had depleted the whole packet of cigarettes.

Fig 22. Wesleyan Church of Hihifo. Photo by Anna Strumillo 4 May 2010.

Tangimana noted the difference between Mum and Dad's treatment of the local people and that by the other ministers. Mum and Dad were relaxed when some people came to 'steal' tava from the trees at night for example. Compare that to one minister who hung sheets of tin from the tava trees so that they clanged noisily when bats or intruders tried to pick their ripe fruits. There were only 4 water tanks in the whole of Niua, 3 were government properties and 1 at the church property. During drought periods, Mafi would let people draw water from the cement tank at their home until it was empty. Other Faifekau wives would turn people away before the tank was empty. Mafi did not mind sharing the tank water and then using coconut milk from young coconuts if there was no more rain water to drink.

There was the story about a big meeting hosted at Vaipoa by the then faifekau, Fisi'ihoi. After the feast, the faifekau's wife, 'Oli, called out to Sione to remember to take with him the basket of food she had packed for him. 'Oli got a real earful from her husband, saying Sione does not carry a basket of food on his bicycle. Later, Tangimana was asked to carry the basket back to Mafi after the meeting. Sione burst out laughing when Tangimana turned up at home with the basket of food.

Dad seemed to have enjoyed Tangimana's helping hand and company. At the end, Tangimana became the Setuata (steward) at the Hihifo Church. He observed that Mafi was very close to Siale Vivili, Paula Vivili's mother. Siale was Mum's right hand help for her women's groups like Kaluseti.

It was with a sad tone of voice that Tangimana told of how the people of Niua missed Sione and Mafi and their ways so very much. People continued to write to them for quite some time after they moved to Kolovai. The replacement faifekau, Semisi Koloto, became quite angry with his congregation when he saw their hearts were longing for Sione and Mafi's presence. He finally implored them to please turn their heart to him and his ministry, as Sione and Mafi have now got another congregation to minister to.

Tangimana concluded regarding how the congregation in NTT felt.

> "Pea 'oku te'eki pe ke lava mato'o 'a e loto 'oe kainga ni mei he ongo matu'a 'ofa mo anga lelei hange ko Sione mo Mafi. Neongo na'e 'iai 'ae kau tu'ukimu'a na'a nau fou atu 'i he hala tatau, ka na'e malava kenau fakafaikehekehe'i 'a e to'onga mo'ui 'oe tangata 'e taha mei he tangata 'e taha."

Translated:

> "Still to this day, we, the people of the Hihifo congregation, pine after this extremely kind and caring couple. We may have had ministers with higher credentials since then, but they could not surpass Sione and Mafi in their way of life nor their Christian discipleship."

CHAPTER 4

Happiness is not something you postpone for the future; it is something you design for the present.
Jim Rohn

KOLOVAI: JULY 1952 – 1955

'Aleki had no recollection of the trip from Niuatoputapu via Vava'u and Ha'apai. He however, had pictures etched in his mind of a truck backing up to the end of the Vuna wharf to receive our personal belongings and ourselves. It was early hours of the morning. Having not heard about trucks, cars etc, it was quite an experience for a young 4 year old boy. The next few days of course would have tripled or quadrupled his general knowledge in the capital island of Tongatapu. The same could be said about the rest of the troupe. Lute and Pesi remember their first taste of ice cream on arrival day. The truck carrying us stopped at Mataele's shop in Nuku'alofa so that Dad could order the children some ice cream in cones. Lute remembers Dad pointing out that the cones should be eaten as well, 'Do not throw it away as it might give us a *luma* (cause for mockery).' Pesi admits that she did not enjoy this *'aisi kilimi* as it made her teeth ache (chewing instead of licking it).

The children remember well the old style colonial wooden building that was the residence of the *Faifekau* at Kolovai. It had a big common room in the centre, 2 large bedrooms on either side of it. At the back of the house were 2 smaller multi-functional rooms and a separate dining room. One of these back rooms was normally used for preparing food like bread-making and for food storage: yams, peanuts, water melons etc. The other was used by the children as a play room, or to sleep visitors. Mafi's brother Hanipale and Dad's brother Tevita and their families took turns visiting us regularly at Kolovai. There was a concrete water tank beside the house on the left side.

An outhouse for cooking the food over an open fire (and in which the underground oven would go) was on one side of this 'peito'. According to Dad, for the first time in his various missions, he received a *'Loma'* and not a *'Saliote ngāue'* (full sized cart). The Loma was lighter and had more flexible springs, making the job of pulling it lighter work for the horse and for the riders, and taking a much shorter time to reach the destination. It gave the riders a much more comfortable experience as well.

The Toa trees (casuarina) in front of the property on most days evicted a strange mixture of sounds like the whistle of wind against fibrous leaves, the quackish-hawkish sound of adult bats thinned by the whistling effort at sound making by infant bats. Sometimes, 'Aleki found an infant bat on the grass under the trees. He tied one of the legs to a branch of a small tree beside the house with a string and tried to raise the infant bat with ripe bananas and leftovers from our meals. They did not reach adulthood under his care.

The fact that the baby flying foxes did not survive under 'Aleki's care is to be expected as these fruit bats are nocturnal mammals. They are normally in their mothers' pouches sucking milk for their early sustenance. Fruit bats are often highly dangerous to humans as they may carry diseases like rabies, flu viruses and fungal disease histoplasmosis. If other mammals, including humans, are bitten by a rabies infected bat, they would certainly die from it unless they are given anti-rabies injection immediately. The infected bat would also die from their disease as well.

There is a folklore about how flying foxes came to be at Kolovai. A Samoan Princess gifted a Tongan Prince two flying foxes which he brought to his home at Kolovai. The flying foxes are sacred and protected by the Royal family. Only they can hunt these flying foxes.

This was the exact house where our parents, Sione Finau and Mafi Helu got married in 1942. We only found this out in Melbourne from Siupeli Taliai in 2016 at his 90th birthday. Siupeli is the only son of Rev 'Ikani and Neomai Taliai.

The site of this building is labelled Cokevernal (Kokanavela) in Pesi Fonua's Walking Tour map of Kolovai. According to Helen Woodgate Taliai, this was the name originally given to the Mu'a Mission by Walter Lawry in 1822.

At Kolovai, there is an enclosure where the former Tu'i Kanokupolus were invested. A piece of the koka tree under which these Kings sat on their investiture is now embedded in the modern coronation chair in Nuku'alofa. The tombs of these kings are also at Kolovai in the Pouvalu (8 posts) Cemetery.

The trench running perpendicular to the road (Hala Hihifo) on the southern part of the property was a source of fun to all of the children during periods of heavy rain. Faka'uha (rain bath) was definitely huge fun but this was something even better. We would grab coconut frond midribs to skate, skid or slide down the steep and very muddy slope of the trench. It was only later that we discovered the trenches were excavated during the dark and treacherous Tongan Civil Wars that characterised the late 18th and early 19th centuries.

'Aleki recalled

One of the first major projects that Dad and I embarked on was to refurbish our residence. We went on the *Loma* and harvested some choice bamboo sticks from someone's *'api 'uta*. We laid the bamboo sticks on the ground and used 2 posts to pound the bamboo sticks until they were completely flattened. We then wove half of the flattened sticks through the other half of them. Three such walls were produced which were then attached to the veranda to provide an extra enclosed area. We repeated this process about every two years.

**Fig 23. Sleeping flying foxes in Kolovai.
Photo by Anita of CNN Sept 2014**

The church *'api 'uta* at this posting was beside the sea on the right of where the Good Samaritan Resort stands now. Here, Sione and I grew our annual yam plot, then on harvest, replanted with sweet potato, then *talo futuna* then cassava, interspersed with banana (*siaine* and *hopa*) and talo Tonga. We would rotate the planting the next year to ensure enough rich organic matter to the demanding yam crop. Certain Saturdays Dad, Viliami (after he joined our family) and I would do some work on the plot then go to the beach to use the fish net (*kupenga sili*). We cooked some of the catch on coals and took the rest home for cooking in the evening or in the Sunday *'umu*.

Net casting is a skill that develops with use. It involves simultaneously, the use of feel, sense, and vision to find the target, cast the net and step in quickly for the kill.

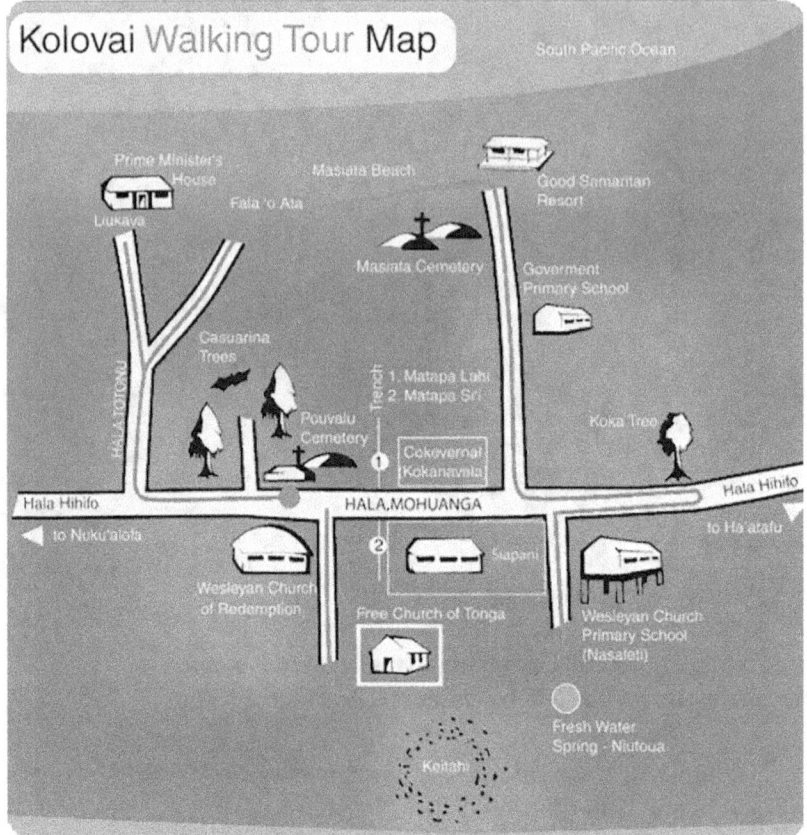

Fig 24. From Pesi Fonua's Walking Tour map. The Prime Minister's House was built for Lavaka. Since he became H.M. King Tupou VI, his youngest son, Ata, now resides in this house.

Sione also inherited a 10 acre block of land from his father Muni, at 'Utulau. Muni (Viliami) was in a small group of farmers that Tungi Mailefihi (Prince Consort to Queen Sālote) formed. They showcased their yams each year. Tungi Mailefihi owned most of the farming land of 'Utulau. He gave each of the five in the group 10 acres of land to use and to keep.

The Loma came in very handy because it made the long trips to and from that *'api* shorter and more comfortable. The trip sometimes started on Friday afternoon after school, spent the night there in a hut we constructed from branches and coconut leaves. We would wake up early, make an 'umu, do some work like hoeing (weeding), digging and planting, collecting coconuts for cooking back at home, harvesting yams, taro, bananas, sweet potato etc. We ate lunch and worked some more. Loading up the Loma was next. Everything from coconuts, vegetables, firewood and banana leaves for wrapping parcels like *lu pulu*, were piled on to the Loma. We would get back to Kolovai late in the evening on Saturday. There were many *'apis* here in 'Utulau which together formed a very good environment for wild fowls (moa kaivao). I thought Dad was a skilful trapper. His best result was 8 hens and roosters. The *'Aa hiki* (trap) consisted of a traylike contraption made of sticks and chicken wire. The contraption was held off the ground by an indented stick with a string tied to each end and through the cut (indent) in the stick. A split coconut was left inside the contraption. The chickens on entering broke the stick in two and the contraption fell and trapped the unsuspecting chickens. Animal husbandry was an important part of family life and I, 'Aleki, was involved intimately in these tasks now. Dad, Viliami and I, had always taken core members of our pig herds and chicken flocks with the family when it was time to move to the next station. Viliami and I were tasked clearly with getting enough coconuts from our allotments to supplement the leftover feeds for the pigs and chickens. When young male pigs were about 8 or so weeks old, we would confine them in a fence, catch the young ones and castrate them. One developed quite good skills in catching the animals when giving them their feed. Sometimes, sows were run down in condition requiring separate feeding and medication, for control of internal and external parasites. We would sometimes need to capture pigs and chickens for cooking for special occasions or to take to hospital to feed sick relatives for example.

Lu pulu is a delicacy in Tonga that is made from young leaves of the taro futuna plants, coconut cream, and corned beef then wrapped up in a wilted banana leaf. This is cooked in an 'umu for the best result.

In all residences, the girls' room had a double and a single bed. Mosiana and Lute slept in the double bed and Pesi in the single.

Both beds had mosquito nets as mosquitoes buzzed around our ears without the nets. Most doors and windows needed to be left open most of the time to allow for cool breezes through the house.

Some of Pesi's memories

Pesi has fond memories of the front garden under the veranda in Kolovai. She helped mum plant packs of pereannial seeds: *potolaka*, *pula* (petunias), *mangiki* (forget-me-nots), fragrant *kalonikali*, *hone* (chrysanthimums), *melekoula* (marigolds), *lile* (lilies), *talia* (dahlias) etc. Pesi loved weeding the garden with Mum, and she kept that up in Ma'ufanga and Vaini. Kalonikakala is a creeper, having smallish red flowers in bunches and has the best perfume by far of all fragrant flowers we had in our various homes. Unfortunately, the plant had huge caterpillars found all over its leaves during its flowering season. They ensured none of us picked its flowers. Ugh!

Morning and evening prayers were said every day before breakfast and dinner. Breakfast consisted of homemade bread, butter and home-made jam. We walked home from school for a hot lunch of mainly vegetables with leaves and a small portion of meat cooked in coconut cream. Sometimes there would be a stew of some sort. Mum and Dad would chat in English if they did not want us to understand certain conversational topics. This became less frequent as we grew up and our English improved.

PLAYTIME

After school, some days the neighbour's children, especially Nesi from Sina's house, would go with us girls to their *'api'uta* or ours to collect quavas, pawpaw, oranges, mandarins, *tava* (lychees) or pineapples. We threw *talatala* (lantana) flowers on the gigantic spider webs then wrapped them up to form garlands. We would make leis from frangipani flowers. We held up our skirts to fill with our pickings and marched home singing in a single file. Our playmates included Sione Mo'unga and Taufa's children Likupaongo,

Sepiuta, and Vinolia. From Sina and Lepolo's household came Nesi, Manutu'ufanga and Kelepi. Latukefu and Vaimoana's children were mostly much older than us. Only Tupou and Lesoni came to play with us sometimes. Lupeti and Mele Mo'ungaloa Finau's children often joined us when they visited from Nukunuku. They were Lavinia and Fale'aka Finau. Our favourite games played at Kolovai were similar to those in Hihifo, Niuatoputapu with the addition of skipping, knucklebones, hopscotch, climbing trees, and marbles. Some of these playmates like Likupaongo Mo'ungaloa Niumeitolu, Sepiuta Mo'ungaloa Fotofili and Fale'aka Finau Taumoepeau are now living in Sydney. Many of the Latukefu clan are living in Canberra, ACT and Queanbeyan, NSW. Their eldest son, Dr Sione Latukefu, lived with his family in Canberra till he passed away. Tevita, Talia'uli and Maile have passed away as well. Maile's wife Lesieli Latukefu, is living in Sydney. Lesoni, the youngest brother married Lu'isa Ma'ilei from Pea (ex THS student in 'Aleki's year) and they live in Canberra, ACT. Lesoni is now Latukefu.

Fig 25. At Kolovai Tongatapu. l-r: Sione Latukefu Teacher Feletoa Vailea, Jan Gammage, Alopi Latukefu. 5 February 1975.

Mafi loved seafoods. She and the girls would often go to the lagoon (eastern beach) to look for crabs, *kaloa'a* (bivalve shellfish), *to'o* (pipis), *'elili* (sea snails), sea cucumbers, sea urchins, jellyfish etc. When the tide was out, most shellfish (bivalves), crabs etc would be semi exposed, however some, like jellyfish, would be floating in the deeper water. Mafi would often venture into this section in search of *jellyfish* and other seafoods.

The beach on the western side had a reef running parallel to the beautiful sandy shore and was further away from home. This was where Dad, 'Aleki and Viliami went net fishing (sili) sometimes after attending to the vegetable garden. It had beautiful sparkling blue waterholes that were heavenly to swim in when the tide was out and were home to big 'elilis (seasnails) and some crabs. Families and schools used this beach for picnics and fishing in the 1950s.

Fig 26. The beautiful Kolovai western beach at high tide

For all our growing up years, everyone in Tonga attended Sunday morning church after preparing lunch. 'Aleki viewed the Sunday routine as necessity for children of a Faifekau. It necessitated children to attend the Sunday service in the morning and then turn up to Sunday school after a heavy lunch. His take on them was: they were not always events to look forward to. Because of where we were seated, we were highlighted (meaning we always had to be at our best behaviour). He did not think that it was the gravity of the religious proceedings that made them unattractive to him. Rather, the boring nature of the routine, which made little change to procedures, interpretations and teaching style over time. This was the major cause of 'Aleki's complaints. Sitting through long sermons was like torture. He recollected, 'The true nature of young children, including, fidgeting and running around, were being repressed. Sometimes, violence was dished out by the doorkeeper who kept a walking stick by his side, invariably waving it to warn the kids against their natural inclination.' While we were at Kolovai, Dad's brother, Tevita was sacked from his job as a prison guard. Tevita was looking after some prisoners outside *Teufaiva* (Tonga's major rugby/sports/show ground) while a game was on. He failed to restrain the prisoners from climbing trees and peering over the fence at the rugby game. His family came home where Dad proceeded to reprimand his brother and then to help him plan his future. Dad then asked Tevita to move back to Lofanga with his family, take on the family title, Muni (which normally would be Dad's) and use our family *'api 'uta* to support themselves. He was to build a house at the *'api kolo*.

**Fig 27. The new Kolovai Wesleyan Church
(built to the style of the old church).**

At that stage, Tevita and his wife Mele had five children: Uaafe, Lilieta, Viliami, Seini and Mafi. Mele and the girls were all fair and lovely looking. Tevita and Mele went on to add five more children to their brood: Sione, Suli, Heilala, Fipee and 'Ofa. Most of these cousins are married and live in USA. Muni (Tevita) passed away in 1990, and Mele only passed away in 2011. Their son, Sione, married 'Una and they have settled in Palmerston North, New Zealand.

'Aleki continued

The girls started school immediately the family arrived in Kolovai. I formally went to primary school here. It was not long before my cousin, Viliami, joined me in primary school. I was the same age as Viliami and I was so very proud of my strong looking cousin. The second day of Viliami's attendance at school, I got him to fight with the school bully. Viliami beat him up. On the third day, my cousin overstepped the mark. Viliami fought someone smaller than him but with far better street fighting skills. I had to take my cousin home badly bruised physically and perhaps more damagingly, psychologically. Of course, we learnt later in life that we can achieve much more through negotiations rather than confrontations.

Lute and Pesi remember

At night on most weekdays, Dad held homework classes of Maths, English, Spelling for the older children. He coached his three older girls for the entrance exams to THS and QSC. THS had a strict age limit of under twelve years old and only accepted the top 20 students from the examinees. Actually, this number was rather flexible later on as some first intake classes had 22 or 23 students, from Pesi's observation.

Mosiana started at QSC in 1955 and she boarded at the College and came home at the weekends, like Dad and Mum in their time. Of all her time at QSC, Head Tutor, Liu Tongilava, a very close friend of

Mafi's, and a relative of Dad's, kept a close eye on Mosiana. Her bed was kept next door to Liu's bed for all her time at QSC.

The primary school Principal, Samipeni, decided to give Pesi a chance to try out at the THS entrance exam while 9 years old. Lute was 11 years old and was sitting the exam at the same time.

Lute and Pesi both passed the THS entrance exams at the end of 1955. They caught a converted truck, the mode of people transport at the time, to THS each morning. After school, they would wait for the truck under the hibiscus hedge of the QSC *Faifekau's* home next door to THS. Unfortunately, there was no set timetable for the transport truck. Some afternoons, no truck came past our waiting spot. Our parents organised emergency arrangements to cover such situations. The Methodist Minister in charge of QSC was our mum's cousin, Rev Latu Puloka and his wife Sela. Sela was a very close and special friend of Mafi's. There were quite a few nights that Lute and Pesi would ask Sela and Latu Puloka to take us in overnight. Our family are very much indebted to Rev Latu and Sela Puloka and their children, especially Mohenoa (now Rev Dr Mohenoa Puloka) and Mele'ana (now, Rev Dr Mele'ana Puloka) for their hospitality during those times.

Memorable events that Pesi remembers

There were rare occasions of seeing movies at the Fale Kautaha (Town Hall) in Kolovai. These happened after the older girls started at secondary school. They saw mainly Western movies. When Lute and Pesi attended Tonga High School in 1956, the school often fundraised by showing films at Mataele's cinema in Nuku'alofa. The film stars were so prettily or magnificently dressed and the actors were beyond handsome. Cooked unshelled peanuts were a must at the cinemas.

Great excitement took place on the evening of 24th September 1953. Mosiana was asked to fetch our Dad's cousin Taufa, from next door to help. Dr Mangisi was sent for immediately. The new baby boy duly arrived. Meanwhile, Noble Ata's sister, Tominika was a visitor on our front veranda. She was very elderly and used to just wander around in the evenings. She suffered from dementia. Our new baby brother was sent a name from the Noble's household. Our little brother was to be named Latu Vaihumoa. Our parents added Sione to be the baby's first name. Mum and Dad were overjoyed that they had another son and 'Aleki loved having a little brother.

The noble of Kolovai has the title Ata.
These days the title may be given to a
son of the current King or Queen.

When Mafi recuperated from the birth of her new son, she started her series of concerts for her nephew 'Ilaisa Futa Helu. Futa attended THS. His father, Fatai Helu IV and the rest of the Helu family figured he was gifted and decided to send him to Sydney for further education during the early 1950s. All of Lotofoa and Helu families everywhere were asked to help finanacially. Mafi mobilised her girls and some locals to perform dances and their relatives would pin *pa'anga* (pound) notes or throw coins into a big bowl under the dancer's feet. Items of value may also be pinned to the dancer or left on the stage as a mark of appreciation by their family and friends or as donation to the good cause. These could include money, mats, pieces of material etc. Mafi would convert all these gifts to cash and forward it to Australia. One of the dance costumes that Mafi made me was of the pungent smelling marigold flowers. No sweet perfume emanated from these bright yellow flowers from our front garden beds. The girls teased me with it for years after. How could our mother think of such stinky flowers to make my costume, Pesi fumed? Mafi continued to hold these fundraising events wherever we went, until Futa returned to Tonga.

Sefita Hao'uli wrote in Polynesian Paradox. (Essays in Honour of 'I. Futa Helu. University of South Pacific 2005.)

'When the Helu family made the decision in the early 1950s that Futa should leave Tonga to further his education at Newington College in NSW and then Sydney University, there was an expectation in my (Hao'uli) family that we should contribute to the vast cost involved. In those days we would allow Helu family members to help themselves to the mature coconuts in our plantation. They were turned into copra and sold for cash to the Copra Board. It was a small price to pay for a family that had brought *mana* to the whole extended family and to Lotofoa.'

Salesi Tupou and his family were very helpful and became reliable friends of our family. Their home is at the back of the Church Primary School principal's residence. As mentioned in Chapter 2, Salesi's eldest son, Sovea was one of Sione and Mafi's students at Veitongo during World War II.

In 1953, Mafi was desperately ill and required blood transfusion for her operation. Salesi stepped in to donate his blood when needed. No one in our family, at short notice, was found to have matching blood type. We are ever so grateful to Salesi Tupou for saving Mafi's life at that time. 'Aleki wrote that when he returned from studying in Queensland, Australia, Salesi's children were close to him for quite some time. The girls, Siosi and 'Alilia, were particularly close to him. He often shared his meagre salaries with them. The elder son, Sovea, sometimes attended kava parties with 'Aleki.

At home with Mum and Dad

Dad worked very hard delivering sermons every Sunday, attending meetings, conferences and so on. He would ride his bicycle to different places to visit his congregation, conduct funerals, weddings and christenings. He would preside over festivities and make speeches. These are on top of helping at home with gardening and tending the pigs and poultry or gardening at the *'api utas* and fishing. Sometimes, relatives like Viliami Sunia from Ha'atafu would come in a truck and drop off big *fua* fish for us.

The tradition with families hosting the Sunday preacher to lunch after church and providing a basket of cooked food for the preacher's home or sending a basket of uncooked food on Saturday to the preacher was a great help to Mafi's budget. She used her cooking skills to make these donations last for as long as possible, in spite of there being no fridge or freezer. Hence the importance of the ability to use preservation methods of meat. Lamb flaps only came into the scene once freezers were introduced to Tonga. Sharing of excess meat around the neighbourhood was the best way to ensure meat was fresh and the population maintained their nutritional requirements.

Mum had her hands full. What with cooking bread and preparing 3 meals a day. When we started at THS, Mum would wake up at 4 am to boil the kettle for the bathroom and our breakfast. She would prepare cooked lunch of *'ufi*, and whatever *kiki* she could find. *Kiki* could be taro leaves, cabbage, tomatoes and/or pele mixed with coconut cream and some meat of some sort if available. Our lunches would be packed in a billy. A second one was often taken for Mosiana at QSC. Mosiana said that her billy was a cause of many fights between her friends. With the growing family, there were more clothes to wash and iron. Mafi washed down our out-toilet every weekend and constantly poured buckets of ash from the fireplace down the pit to minimise unpleasantness. No other households performed this routine from our knowledge.

'Aleki as a young man, visited Kolovai

When I, 'Aleki, was Head of Livestock Division, Head of Advisory and Livestock and Head of Research and Extension at the Ministry of Agriculture and Forestry (M.A.F.) in Tonga, I had many opportunities to share experiences with the people of Hihifo, including Kolovai. The M.A.F. Office for the district was located at Fo'ui. I would spend many consecutive days in the district, inspecting town (with women folks) and tax allotments (with District officers and prominent farmers). My last visit to the Kolovai Faifekau residence was just before I left Tonga to live in Auckland (2000). I visited the Faifekau residence with Mrs Vao Langi Faluku and her women's group. They were showcasing the different 'kakala' plants of Tonga, including langakali, heilala, kalonikakala, pipi, mohokoi etc. The new house was bigger than the one I remembered but the layout was the same and the physical characteristics remained the same.

I thought that the people of Kolovai still had the basic stuff that makes the true warrior (as amply demonstrated in rugby), which, mixed with the fact that their paramount Chief, Ata, accepted Christianity before many other parts of Tonga, gave that special twist to what they accept as their true character, civilised people of strong moral character. I had a special liking to spending time in kava parties at Hihifo, including Kolovai.

Fig 28. A typical Tongan home in Kolovai in the 1950s.

CHAPTER 5

*Start by doing what's necessary,
then do what's possible; and suddenly you are doing what's impossible.
Francis of Assisi.*

HOUMA 1956-1957

The parsonage at Houma was at the geographical centre of the town. It was a smaller town compared to Kolovai, nearer Nuku'alofa by a crow's fly, but it felt more isolated in many ways. Gone were the days of free play after school. The grounds of this home were smaller and there were no big trees surrounding the block. The house was screened from the street by kalakala'apusi (a row of tall red leaved shrubs, it's flowers looked like cats tails). On the left of our house was the town cemetery, surrounded by Toa trees. However there were no screeching flying foxes here.

Later, Mum attempted to grow her perennials along the front of the house but this garden was never that successful. The soil here may not have been suitable. It could have been too salty as we were only about 500 metres away from the famous blowholes. Mafi was still not fully recovered after her major operation in the previous year so she may not have been strong enough to work on the garden as well as complete all the other tasks she needed to perform daily.

Fig 29. Houma Blowholes

Fig 30. Rev Sione Finau and Mafi Helu Sisifa outside our front veranda which had woven coconut fronds to provide a shield against rain and hot sun. 1957.

Diagonally across the road from our house was the church and behind it was the Church Primary School. Beside the church and school compounds on one side and Lei Finau's *'api kolo* on the other side, was an unmade road leading to the swimming beach. Lei Finau, originally from 'Ahau in Hihifo, married a girl in Houma and was given a large 'api kolo and 'api 'uta. Mafi's sister, Meliana, married Lei's eldest son, Mahe Finau. Lei had 3 other children: daughters, Ika Hokafonu and Faapuiaki; and son, Tutulu.

Mahe and Meliana's children were Soana Finau (f,deceased, USA), Kitione Hanipale (m), Sikipio Finau (m, USA), Nanuma Finau Ake(f, deceased June 2018) and Penisimani Finau (m, NZ).

HOME LIFE

Compared to Kolovai, life was slow and rather dull at Houma. Mosiana was now at boarding school again except for her Saturday leave. Lute and Pesi travelled to Nuku'alofa daily to attend THS. There were no children of our age in the vicinity that we could coopt to play with us. On top of that, Lute and Pesi had no time during weekdays with the long travel times and homework to attend to.

While in Houma, measles struck our household. Pesi remembers that the whole tribe was laid low all at the same time. She can still sniff the body odour exuding from her spotted skin. Mum would change sheets, give us drinks, wipe our foreheads, and give us tablets for days. The polio epidemic also hit Tonga during this period. Pesi recalls THS being called to a special assembly whereby the students were informed of the first detection of the debilitating infectious virus poliomyelitis in Tonga. The importance of limiting it's spread was emphasized and then the school was dismissed. The school was closed down for a few weeks. Our family was spared this debilitating virus. The only one affected in our extended family was Tevita 'Ofa Helu, a cousin who attended THS at the time. Fortunately, he was not too severely affected.

Fig 31. Sunset at the Swimming Beach at Houma

T. Ofa Helu continued at THS when he recovered. He went on a Scholarship to Auckland Boys Grammar and then Auckland University in NZ. On his return, he was a lecturer at 'Atenisi University under Professor 'Ilaisa Futa Helu.

'Aleki attended the Church Primary School. Samipeni Maumau was again the school principal working with our parents. Dad and Mum became very close to Samipeni and his wife Sela in Houma. They were also good friends with the bachelor teachers who lived besides the school.

Mafi was a leader in women's affairs. She encouraged women to participate in Kaluseti, the church women's fellowship group. It fostered prayer and spiritual growth for women. She encouraged all women from the church to attend HM Queen Sālote's newly formed Langa Fonua 'a Fefine Tonga.

Mum was active in this association right up to when I left for New Zealand at the beginning of 1962. She attended meetings at Queen Sālote College to help instruct other women folks on preparing nutritious foods for their families and how to keep their homes orderly and clean. The women learnt to make handcrafts from the raw materials they normally used for making mats and tapa cloths. These would then be sold at tourist spots. Pesi remembers attending the Langa Fonua 'a Fefine Tonga Shows (Sou 'a e Langa Fonua) at the grounds of the Church Primary School in Nuku'alofa for many years. Our Mum would make bread, cakes, jam, sweets and handcrafts for these shows. They were enjoyable bazaars, with lots of goodies to eat.

Pesi often visited retired Principal of QSC, Ms Dilys Rowlands, from 2002 to March 2005, at the Andrew Kerr Nursing Home in Mornington, Victoria, Australia, where David Weir (Pesi's husband) was cared for. Pesi learnt from Dilys Rowlands that she had monthly meetings with HM Queen Sālote, and one of their various topics of conversation was the formation of Langa Fonua 'a Fefine Tonga.

Pesi Maumau, daughter of Samipeni and Sela Maumau happily recounted her memories of Sione and Mafi to Lute and Mele Moala in June 2004.

Fig 32. Display at a Langafonua Show

Fig 33. Langafonua

Pesi M. prefaced her stories by saying that even though she was quite young at the time, she remembered Sione and Mafi very clearly. Pesi M. was adopted by Samipeni and Sela. Samipeni graduated with his Maamaloa in 1932. He died at 90 years old in 2002. Sela was present at the interview (aged 89). Sela kept asking whether they really were talking about Mafi and Sione. She said (wiping her tears away) she was very close to Mafi and enjoyed working with her in those days when she was full of energy.

Pesi's job was to take their benzene iron to Mafi on Saturdays. This was easier to use than Mafi's iron which needed hot ash from burnt coconut shells to operate. Electricity came to Tonga much later. Pesi M. remembered very well our Dad's welcoming smile and his quiet and peaceful countenance, every time she visited our house. (Unlike the 'coal iron', a benzene iron could be turned on with a switch, instead of waiting to produce coal in a fire-place to get the iron ready for use.)

Samipeni was a local to Houma. He had a large 'api uta with a lot of coconut trees. When Dad explained about the transport problems to get Lute and Pesi into Nuku'alofa for school, Samipeni offered him the liberty of collecting coconuts from his 'api 'uta to help with fundraising for the girls' transport. Often, Samipeni, lent his Loma to Dad and Mafi on the occasions when Mafi wanted to visit her sister Numia Taloa in Vaini.

Mafi organised local exhibitions of cooking and crafts for Hou ma and the surrounding villages. They were held at Ika Hokafonu's home. Pesi M. proudly related a story by Sela of how she won the 'topai' cooking competition. Mafi had shown her how to add baking powder to the dough mix. Mafi taught the women how to make boiled pulini (boiled pudding) as well as how to vary their cooking from the basic traditional foods.

Fig 34. One of the Langafonua Shows.

Pesi M. remembered how her dad Samipeni was so happy when Mafi made him a suit, a kote and tupenu fakafisi like that worn by Dad in fig 30. She also witnessed Lute and Pesi Sisifa riding their bicycles passed their house, on their way to and from THS. She added that it was very rare for people to own a bicycle, a cart or a Loma. She remembered that 'Aleki, Mele and Latu were very young at the time.

SCHOOL LIFE

Transport into Nuku'alofa was a problem right from the beginning when we arrived in Houma. As mentioned before, Mosiana was at the QSC boarding school. Lute and Pesi were put on the public transport (truck) in the morning. Often, the truck would be overloaded. The girls were regularly stranded in Nuku'alofa at the end of the day. They used Sela and Rev Latu Puloka's home as their emergency accommodation again like when the family was at Kolovai. Mum and Dad decided that the solution for their predicament was bicycles. This presented two extra problems. Their finance would be stretched to the limit to purchase two bicycles. Secondly, riding the distance to Nuku'alofa was fraught with danger. How could they protect their girls every day?

Fig 35. Recent photo of Dr Mele'ana Puloka

Lute and Pesi explain

Mum and Dad decided to send their girls to Lotofoa to Mum's brother Hanipale. He was asked to collect coconuts from the family 'api 'uta and produce copra for the girls. How were the girls getting to Lotofoa? By boat of course. Who would accompany them on the boat? Lute and Pesi were in Form 2. Pesi was 11 and Lute was 13 years old. Mum and Dad approached one of the bachelor teachers at the Church Primary School, Feletoa Vailea (Fig 25), to accompany the girls on their boat journey. Thinking back, Mum and Dad must have prayed a lot during that trip, having sent their daughters away with a male non-relative as chaperone and over all those kilometres in a small boat!

This trip was an absolutely wonderful experience for the girls. On the first port of call at Ha'apai, Nomuka, they met their Dad's cousin, Dr Posesi Fanua. He was the current medical doctor at Ha'apai. He and a team of nurses were at the beginning of a tour of the Ha'apai group of islands to check and attend to the medical health of the local communities. What a coincidence! The medical team and the girls were housed at the Government resident for visiting medical staff. They were well fed by the grateful locals with their best harvests. Every lunch and dinner, there were *tunu* (baskets made from fresh coconut fronds and filled with a variety of cooked food) provided by the local people. There were dried octopus cooked in coconut sauce(yum), fish freshly caught and barbecued or roasted in an 'umu and/or luu-pulu. These were accompanied by yam. Yam is considered to be a delicacy. It is not the everyday root vegetable, unlike taro, sweet potato, breadfruit, or tapioca.

Lute and Pesi left the commercial boat here and joined the medical tour until Pangai.

To get to land from our boat, there were outriggers. However, who can resist the absolutely pristine deep blue water, where you can see the white sand at the bottom of it all? The girls swam ashore at every opportunity. They were given a bath and then a repeat of the receiving the locals and their gifts of food. Many of these islands' inhabitants knew their parents or were related to them in some way.

At Lotofoa, the girls were welcomed everywhere. They stayed at Lesieli Helu's house, the main Helu residence. They were invited to dine at aunty Vai's place, and Peau's house (Peau was Siniva's and Fualupe's mother and Mum's step mother). Hanipale and his older boys produced copra for his visiting nieces.

Fig 36. Nomuka beach.

Fig 37. A beach in Lotofoa.

So with the money from Lotofoa and the help from Samipeni Maumau, two brand new ladies' bicycles were purchased. Dad informed all villages from Houma to Nuku'alofa to watch out for his daughters who would be riding their bicycles to and from school every day. For the remaining years of our stay in Houma, Lute and Pesi rode their bicycles to and from THS. Half way from home to

THS lived a palangi girl called Daphne whose parents managed a cattle and coconut farm. When her family learnt of the THS girls' mode of transport, they asked if Daphne could join them. This was great because on the way home from school, Lute and Pesi would have a snack and drink at Daphne's house before completing their journey. There was never any untoward incident in all their riding time. Pesi met a Tongan lady at a dance in Canberra in 1994 who when she found out that Sione Sisifa was her Dad, she related how her whole village used to marvel at Sione's clever children riding past their village every day. She said they had never seen THS students before!

Fig 38. THS 1957 Form 2 class in front of the small staff room.

3rd row: Sione Liava'a, Sione Havea, Ati Ikakoula, Lapulou Lutui, Saane Taumoepeau, Lavili, Nita Manu, Moala Naitoko, Hola Fotu, Simione Fatafehi. 2nd row: Mr Paul Bloomfield, Leafa Tuita, Kelela Loiti, Vika Havea, Langitoto Niuafe, Kakala, Pesi Sisifa, Lotolua 'Alatini, Lute Sisifa, (Wailangilala Tufui, Losaline Fakatou absent). 1st row: Mosese 'Aholelei, Pita Manilala, Kuli Ha'apai, Sione Talanoa, Maka Tu'akoi, Roy Cocker, Sione Tu'i'ile'ila, Home Guard Mailau.

Mum continued to get up early to get her children's breakfast and to cook their lunch. They carried their lunch in their pili (tin container). Mosiana got her pili of food as well at boarding school. At THS, most children would go home for lunch as most students lived in Nuku'alofa. The few students from villages would go to the main shops to look for doughnuts at Manilala's shop. There were not many restaurants or take away cafes at the time. Street stalls only sold doughnuts, peanuts, and green coconuts. When Dad came into Nuku'alofa on church affairs, he would drop by at school to give his girls 5 cents each. With this Pesi could buy lollies or a doughnut. She remembers how one year she was very pleased with herself. She saved up her money and bought Dad some tobacco for Christmas after he had been trying to quit for a month or two. He was most appreciative at the time. On hindsight, Pesi did him no favour at all. Mum must have been unhappy that he went back to smoking again. It was here that Mum began having Christmas trees for the children.

WEEK-END PLAY

The children often played card games here in Houma. They played skipping a lot at school and at home. They also started to play tennis. Mosiana says she looked forward to the weekends to return home from QSC to play tennis with her siblings. On a few occasions they were allowed to go swimming at the safe swimming beach.

They were often allowed to travel to Tokomololo during their school holidays. Their aunt 'Ana Mo'unga (Mafi's sister) lived there with her Fijian husband, Latu Paa, surrounded by fruit trees, vegetable gardens with avocados, pawpaw, oranges, tava trees and pineapple plants. They had a small Tongan/Fijian house. Life was very simple and free of any pretence. Latu Paa used to spend a lot of time at the Palace of HM Queen Sālote, helping to receive her majesty's visitors. The children never encountered him at home. Their days there were complete free play among the trees and chickens. Their cousins that lived with 'Ana were Hanipale's children: Seini and Losipeli Helu. Losipeli taught his visitors how to climb fruit trees, catch chickens for lunch by out-running them. In the evenings, he showed his visiting cousins how to gently push a fowl off its perch on the mango tree, on to an upside down half coconut shell on a pole, while the birds were asleep. They learnt to hold their breath and lower the pole gently but quickly.

Losipeli Helu later went back to Foa, Ha'apai, with his family. Tu'ipelehake of that time (nephew of HM, King Tupou IV), bestowed on him the title Helu VI. At the time, most of Sioeli Helu's children and grandchildren were in Tongatapu, Auckland or Sydney. Losipeli was hard-working and obviously had leadership qualities inspite of being handicapped with having lost one leg when very young.

CHURCH LIFE

On occasions, Noble Vaea, his wife, Tuputupu, (later Lord Vaea and Lady Tuputupu) and his family would attend Sunday service. This is where Pesi first saw their daughter Nanasi. Years later (1995, after she married the King's youngest son), Pesi sat next to Nanasi at an International Womens' Day Breakfast in Canberra. As the President of the Women's Club, Zonta, ACT, Pesi helped organise the day and made the welcoming speech to the speaker, Ita Buttrose. Pesi must have shocked Princess Nanasi and her companion, Lavinia Naufahu, when she asked Princess Nanasi at the end of their conversation, who she was!

Princess Nanasi became HM Queen Nanasipau'u of Tonga in 2012. Many weddings were held at the church in Houma. However, Pesi remembers being intrigued by many that were held at the parsonage for couples who eloped because their parents did not approve of the match or were avoiding costly weddings. She supposes looking back, Dad could see that most eloping couples were in love and deserved to be married to each other. Lute says some of these people, years later, would stop her on the road in Nuku'alofa to explain how grateful they were that she helped them marry by signing their marriage certificate at our house some years back. Some explained their reason for marrying that way.

Church Conferences were and still are big church and national events in Tonga. The Royal family always participated fully. Every village/town took turns in feeding those attending the Conference. When the Conference was held at Nuku'alofa, Saione Motu'a, Lute and Pesi often stayed overnight sharing dad's rolled-out bed on the floor, joining in the dinner feasts and in the morning breakfast feasts (polas) before school. The ministers from out of town and outlying islands all slept in dormitory arrangements on the floor of the church primary school buildings which normally surround the Methodist Church building.

Apparently, now these conferences provide free-for-all feeding frenzy for the whole population of wherever it takes place, Tongatapu, Ha'apai or Vava'u. I have heard of busloads of non-Methodists arriving at meal times to participate and to pack doggy bags to take home.

At the 2006 census, about 37% of the population belonged to the Methodist Church (or Free Weslyan Church). 15.6% belong to the Free Church of Tonga, 16.8% belong to Jesus Christ of Latter-day Saints and 11.3% belong to the Roman Catholic Church.

Houma is one of the important centres for the Catholic Church. Unlike many other towns. Pesi suspects half of the town were Catholics when they were there. She cannot recall many church youth activities in Houma except for film evenings held at the primary school building. Rev Sione's next posting, Ma'ufanga, saw a lot of youth participation in church activities that were driven by Rev Sione Finau and Mafi Sisifa.

CHAPTER 6

*One cannot reflect in streaming water. Only those
who know internal peace can give it to others.
Lao Tzu*

MA'UFANGA 1957-1959

Sione and Mafi's older children have very fond memories of Ma'ufanga as a place to live. It had a warm and welcoming feel to it. It was by the beach. Plenty of visitors from other parts of the kingdom called at this parsonage as they travelled by boat to and from Tongatapu.

The Sisifa family was back together again here. THS and QSC were only about 8 km from home. The grounds of this home was not the largest 'api kolo but was still very roomy. The house was set to the left of the block, close to the Church. The right side of the block had many mature coconut trees, and behind them was an extensive vegetable garden of taros, banana trees and tapioca. Huge mango trees of the neighbours' shaded a lot of this garden. The outhouses for the bathroom and loo were among the vegetable garden. This made it difficult for the children to visit them at night. It meant waking someone to accompany you.

The peito was pretty big here. So was the dining outhouse. There was a particularly big dining table here too. The residence had only two but big bedrooms. There were big open front and back verandas. Verandas are suitable for the hot days in Tonga. In hot evenings, the girls would lie on the verandas looking at the stars and talking till it was cool enough to move back into the bedrooms.

The Noble of Ma'ufanga is Fakafanua. As shown on one of Dad's family trees (FT I), two generations back, the eldest son of

Fakafanua, Kisi, gave up his title for love. He married Sione's great grandmother Veisinia, in Lofanga. In Tonga's family tree analysis, we are close relatives of the Fakafanua family.

Lute on Ma'ufanga

This town felt alive and busy compared to Houma. Fāua Wharf was only a few meters from the church residence. It was used as the wharf for the inter-island boats. Ma'ufanga had a big population compared to Houma. In 2007, a new and much bigger wharf was completed along the western side of Fāua Wharf, and was named Queen Salote Wharf. There was a very active Catholic church here as well. The main Catholic Boys School 'Api Fo'ou is located here.

Fig 39. Queen Salote Wharf viewed from East shore looking towards Nuku'alofa. Taken by Andrea Wisener 4 May 2007.

The foreshore of Ma'ufanga has had a huge transformation with the Queen Salote Wharf dwarfing the old Fāua wharf on its east side. In the late 1950s, the Fāua wharf was a dug-out short channel with a built up concrete platform on its right hand side. There was no building/shed there.

Fig 40. Butchering a whale in Ma'ufanga foreshore. (From Helen R. Taliai)

Lute says, 'Nowadays, Ma'ufanga houses the Gas and the Oil supply for Tonga. The majority of industrial businesses and factories are located there.' Ma'ufanga has become quite a hive of business activities.

The girls were old enough here to share in the household chores in the weekends. Pesi remembers being the main cook for the Saturday lunch. This involved cooking the vegetables and stoking the fire. Mum would still make the *kiki*. *Kiki* here sometimes included whale meat. The whale hunters were from the Cook family in Fasi. They were part palangis. A harpooned whale would be towed from where it was caught to beside the wharf. It was cut up into smaller pieces and sold to the public from where it was tethered. Pesi was put off by the red blood that coloured the sea where the whale was butchered, so she never shared in this *kiki*. Shark meat could be bought at a nearby wharf for Government fishing boats. Pesi did not like the smell of this meat so she did not like shark meat either.

At the beginning, Mum would spend hours washing our clothes. Mosiana and Lute were supposed to help her. Mosiana complained a lot when Lute would often be found reading comics instead of helping. Later, a relative from Nomuka called Piula used to help mum with the washing board. He was in his thirties and a big strong man.

There were chickens and ducks wandering around our yard and especially near the *peito*. They ate the grated coconut after the milk was extracted for cooking the vegetables, and scraps of food. Another job that Piula used to do was to shake the yeast mixture that started the bread dough. One day he shook the bottle with the mixture so vigorously that it blew apart gashing a deep cut into his arm. His arm was in a sling for quite a long time. He slept at someone else's home but would come to our house every day to help with the chores.

Fig 41. Mafi's sister, Meliana Helu Finau, with niece Moana Weir, nephew Steven Francis. 2nd row: son Hanipale, niece Mele Moala Aleamotu'a.

Mafi's sister Meliana, often visited with her daughters Soana and Nanuma on some weekends and during some school holidays. Her husband Mahe was working at Nukunuku Church Primary School at the time. Meliana needed to use Mafi's sewing machine to make her girls' new clothes. The girls would invariably stay behind for the school break afterwards. Lute explained that Meliana continued to come to her house to use this sewing machine until around early 1970s. Pesi gave Lute a treading sewing machine then so she passed on Mafi's old sewing machine to Meliana. Meliana, was also an excellent dress maker and had a flair in this department. She delighted in designing clothes and dancing costumes for her daughters.

SCHOOL LIFE

Lute and Pesi shared one bicycle to ride to THS while Mosiana left boarding school and travelled from home instead. She used our lady's bicycle. Lute and Pesi joined Wailangilala and Saane Tufui in Fasi, on our way to THS in the morning. We all rode home to have lunch every day. Pesi remembers at this time, after learning about bacteria in General Science, she hated drinking the water from our water tank. She wanted to drink boiled water or she would climb a leaning young coconut tree which was easy to climb, and pick a young coconut to drink.

Pesi was improving fast at school at about this stage and was getting to the top of her class. Mum and Dad decided that maybe THS was not the right type of school for Lute and it was not good for the girls to be in the same class. Lute changed schools to QSC. She fitted in very well there, topping her class immediately.

Pesi continued to enjoy school immensely. There were assemblies in the mornings under the mango trees in the back or in the quadrangle beside the main building. There were the detentions for being caught speaking in Tongan. If caught, that student had to sweep the grounds, especially under the mango trees. Pesi's classmates were Leafa Tuita Taumoepeau, Vika Havea, Wailangilala Tufui, Langitoto Niuafe, Kelela Loiti, Hola Fotu, and Losaline Vaohingano Fakatou, Mele Lotolua 'Alatini from Hofoa, Lapulou Lutui, Moala Naitoko. Other class mates were Sione Havea, Sione Liava'a, Roy Cocker, Pita Manilala, Sione Talanoa, Mosese 'Aholelei, Irene Cocker, Kuli Ha'apai Faleafa, Simione Fatafehi, Atiluma Ikakoula, and Home Guard Mailau. The classmates that are still around are scattered around the world, in mainly the USA, NZ, Australia, England and Fiji.

One of Pesi's favourite teachers was Mr Shilling from Canada. He taught Maths, Science, and Physical Education. Pesi found Maths particularly fun, especially Geometry. Mr Shilling showed them how to play softball, volleyball and basketball. He took them swimming at the pier at Kolofo'ou. He also got them square-dancing. He organised school socials so that the students could use their square dancing skills. Pesi remembers going off to one of these evenings and Dad saying, 'Remember we do not dance in our church.' Pesi, thought to herself, "Well, so what does he think we will do all evening?" They were fun evenings.

'Aleki sat the THS entrance exam at the end of 1959. When the results came out, his name was not on the list for the 1960 intake. Dad could not believe his eyes. He was so sure that 'Aleki was a top student and the examiners had made a mistake. He approached Kilisimasi 'Aho, the Director of Education then, to apply for 'Aleki's papers to be remarked. Sure enough, 'Aleki had performed very well in the exam. Soon 'Aleki put an end to any doubt as to his ability. His exam results were excellent from year one on. He received academic awards every year right from his first year at THS.

Mosiana and Lute started eyeing boys or vice versa. Some even followed them home. The bicycles would be wheeled home instead of being ridden. There were many good-looking sorts in Ma'ufanga, they were from good homes and did very well at Tupou College and Tonga College (The Govt Boys Secondary school).

The usual concrete rain water tank was outside the girls' bedroom. Many of the neighbours came at all hours of the day to fetch water. It was not unusual to hear people outside our window drawing water from the tank at night. Late one night, Lute felt a hand groping at their blankets through a slightly opened window above their bed. She called out loudly and woke up the rest of us. The person took off but we continued to have nightmares about it for a very long time. Years later, in Australia, Pesi's husband, David, woke her up when she called out loudly in Tongan while asleep. She explained that she was just trying to chase away someone from outside the window!

SPARE TIME

The children's spare time was spent on the beach gathering shellfish or swimming at Fāua wharf. Fāua wharf had pretty murky water because of its coral reef base. Pesi was always scared that a shark might bite her leg off so she did not fully enjoy these swims. They sometimes played cricket in the rain, or just faka'uha (chased each other around getting wet). The children often took turns going net fishing with Dad along the foreshore or at Tukutonga. Tukutonga later became the rubbish dump for Nuku'alofa. Later still, people who were very ill but had no *'api kolo* were able to build thatched huts on this mud flat area. Many of these people are still living there now according to Lute. Noble Fakafanua Kinikini allowed many of them to register these plots of land in their names.

The children remember the fun times they had with Christmas trees. Mum had combs, lollies, crackers, ribbons, hairpins, balloons and other little gifts for us. They remember also staying away from school with fevers at Ma'ufanga. Mum would go to the local nuns' pharmacy to collect tablets at a minimum cost, for her ailing brood.

CHURCH & SOCIAL LIFE

Dad continued to perform his church duties admirably. He had a very active congregation. The families who were the backbone of the town were relatives of the noble Fakafanua Kinikini, like Filimoehala. Fakafanua was a handsome looking young man and had just married Kalo 'Ahome'e, a beautiful young woman of high birth, sister to then Crown Princess Halaevalu Mata'aho. Kalo used to spend a fair bit of time chatting with Mum while Fakafanua chatted to Dad. Fakafanua and Kalo attended church regularly while we were at Ma'ufanga.

Fig 42. The enlarged, renovated Weslyan Church of Ma'ufanga, November, 2018.

Lute and Pesi had a bit of fun trying to recall some of the young people's names

A policeman nextdoor named Taupaki had a son named Kaluseti; mother Vaongana had a son named 'Amanaki; 'Ana and Nehu Filimoehala were girls across the road; Mother Kaati (cousin of Fakafanua) married Tiueti and had a son called Tu'ipulotu Kata; Hinagano (another cousin of Fakafanua) had two gilrs called Siunipa and Lupe Filimoehala; Mele Ula married Vikilani's son; Viliami Takau and sister Kalolaine Takau lived near us.

Fakamee (Sunday school Anniversary, in May) and Christmas celebrations were notable here for the children because they were older and more socially aware. Pesi remembers Mum taking some early Sunday School classes, after preparing the Sunday dinner. Pesi loved it when Mum used felt pictures to represent the people in the biblical stories like Jesus performing miracles and His crucifiction scenes.

Mum took on the task of floral arrangements at church. Our front yard was filled with white and red lilies, mangiki, potolaka, marigolds, etc. Hibiscus and frangipani flowers were not deemed suitable for floral arrangements as they did not last long or the stems were too thick to fit in the vases. If she needed supplementing, Pesi was often sent to Mele Longalei's home or Mele Ula's mother's home on Saturdays for their help. Their gardens were extensive and they always had some type of flower blooming.

Mele Longalei, aged 74 on June 18, 2004 recounted to Lute and Mele Moala her very fond memories of Sione and Mafi Sisifa

The thing that stood out to her about Sione was the importance of educating his children. For Mafi, it was her impeccable character (*'ulungaanga*). She was of a different league altogether to all other ministers' wives. She was always so wrapped up in her own family. Mafi concentrated on attending to her husband and children that she had no time for idle chatting. When our Ma'ufanga community observed their behaviour they all put it down to their having grown up in Haapai (no wonder as they came from Ha'apai).

Mafi was extremely organised. The children's school uniforms were spotless. Meals were on time and well prepared, both morning and evening. One evening Mele L. happened to call at the Minister's home when they were about to have their evening meal, she was amazed at the orderliness of the table setting for both parents and the 6 children. There was even a cover over the served food. In 1957, there were not many families that ate together or even managed to have a table and chairs to fit all the family in one sitting. It was/is quite normal to have a few sittings for a meal. The more senior or 'important' members of a family would have their meal first, next important members and then the majority of children last.

Mele L. is another person who remembers Sione as a smiley person. She considered Sione to be a very efficient and professional administrator. He had an easy manner and was very approachable.

He always appeared calm and collected and well prepared in all his programmes for his congregation.

She remembered how Sione constantly stressed in his ministry, the importance of being conciliatory, patient, living peacefully and helping each other in their daily lives. She observed that these traits were exactly how Sione and Mafi were living. She never once saw them exchange a cross word with each other. It was not for lack of opportunity to observe on Mele's part. She claimed that throughout their time in Ma'ufanga, *na'a ne fiu hono lama ha taimi ke ongona mai 'oku na alea le'o lahi, 'oku 'ikai pē* (despite her watching them closely, she never ever observed discord in their family life).

Mafi managed her family's housekeeping finances frugally. Mele L. saw how Mafi managed their everyday living, stretching whatever they had so that they could eat well every day. Mafi and Sione managed to pay the children's school fees and clothe everyone well. She saw Mafi selling the extra fish that Sione caught from his 'sili' or net fishing. Sione further supplemented their income with making copra from the 'api 'utas.

Lute adds that she remembers that at the beginning when the extra fish needed to be sold, she and Pesi one day were sent out on their bicycle to sell the strings of fish. The fish seller is meant to blow a whistle at regular intervals, as he/she pedalled slowly along the street. Lute and Pesi, on the other hand, thought it was unbecoming of them to sell fish.

Fig 43. Church Women's Group 1958.
Back row from left: Finau Takau, Kaati Kata, Kolotina Helu, Mele Longalei, front row: Kalolaine Takau, friend and, Longolongo Kilifitoni Quensell.

They hopped on the bicycle, blew the whistle softly once, then Lute pedalled as fast as she could to the other end of Ma'ufanga. They then came home to tell Mum the sad news. They did not sell any because they were too embarrassed to sell fish on the street. Poor Mum, she had to get one of her cousin's sons, Sioeli from Tokomololo to help her sell her extra fish.

According to Mele L., Sione and Mafi were exemplary, setting a very high standard for their congregation to follow in their daily lives. Mele L. said, 'Even with many years gone by, I can still remember them fondly and vividly.'

Mele L.'s daughter, Eseta Longalei, married Dr Setaleki Finau later, both ex THS students. 'Eseta and Setaleki have settled in Auckland for many years. 'Eseta is a nurse and a very active member of the THS Ex Students Association. She is an excellent communicator and leader in the Tongan and Pacific Island Nursing community in the South Pacific. Setaleki had many medical posts in Tonga, Australia and New Zealand and he took on many leadership roles in Auckland for Pacific Islanders. He is now retired in Auckland.

VISITORS FROM HA'APAI AND VAVA'U

All of the children recall the continuous flow of visitors from the outer islands. These visitors ranged from relatives to church people arriving or returning home from Church Conferences. Some travellers were Church Ministers, teachers, or *setuata* (stewards or persons who do all the menial jobs in caring for a church). Others could be travelling on civil or Government matters. Arriving travellers would stop over at our home to await their transport to where they will stay. Outward travellers would come to wait for the inclement weather to clear before they could sail home. These visitors could stay up to a week at a time. Lute says she always looked forward to the visitors from Ha'apai. They often brought with them: dried octopus, dried fish, turtle, yams and so on. The children remember well the visitors' beds of mats and tapa cloths rolled out in the evening on the verandas or sitting room.

Lute and Pesi further remember how Mafi made arrangements with the local shop of Pili 'Initia to sell her jam tarts and scones to raise more cash. Pesi remembers running the errands for this venture, willingly, without any hesitation. Pili 'Initia and his wife raised a daughter called Peti. She became Noble Ma'afu's wife. Noble Ma'afu is the Noble of Vaini.

At the Church Conference of 1959, Sione and Mafi were posted to Vaini. All belongings were loaded on a huge truck for our move in early 1960. Just as the truck was about to leave, another truck pulled up alongside it. It had all sorts of *'koloa'* (mats and tapa cloths) loaded on it. The Ma'ufanga community was wanting to give his family some thank you gifts. Dad thanked the church community very much and told them his family could not possibly take them. So Sione and Mafi said goodbye again to a community that had grown to appreciate them very much and found it difficult to part with them.

Fig 44. Yacht mooring at the modern Queen Salote Wharf. (There were no such yacht mooring in the 1950s.)

CHAPTER 7

As we express our gratitude, we must never forget that the highest appreciation is not to utter words but to live by them.
John F. Kennedy

VAINI 1960–1962

Arriving at Vaini, Pesi felt it was quite homely. This feeling could have been because Mum and her children had visited Vaini a few times before to see Mafi's eldest sister, Numia Helu Taloa.

Numia and her husband Taloa, had 5 adult children and 3 younger boys at the time. They had a granddaughter our age, Tiulipe. We loved visiting Numia's house because she always spoilt us. She would get the younger boys to cook us yam and complemented the *haka 'ufi* with a tin of corn beef from the general store next door, belonging to 'Iunisi Taufa's parents. 'Iunisi Taufa attended THS and QSC at the same time as Lute. Later on, Lute said the Taloa family opened their own store at the front of their house.

Taloa and Numia's children were: Tu'utanga (f), Taufa (f), Pouono (f), Mahe(m), Pinomi(m), Feke'ila(m), Muli(m), Penisimani(m). Many of them and their families are now spread out in USA, New Zealand and Australia. The only ones still residing in Vaini at the family home are some of Pinomi's children.

Taloa was quite well-to-do, according to the Tongan standard. He had a large *'api 'uta* and a big town block (*'api kolo*). His boys worked the land well so that they wanted for nothing. There were plenty of vegetables and plenty of pigs and chickens. Our uncle, Dr Kuli Helu, sometimes sent his children from Fasi to come and ask for *feta'aki* (partly processed tapa cloth, sometimes used by artists instead of paper), yams etc from his cousin Numia. As soon as we were settled into our new home, Numia sent her granddaughter Tiulipe to come every Saturday to do our washing since she knew Mafi was not strong physically at this stage.

'Iteni Helu (Dr Kuli Helu's eldest son) recalled. June 2004

Fig 45. Mafi's eldest sister, Numia Taloa 1967.

'Iteni said, 'My parents have high regards for Mafi because of her loving and caring nature.' He first met Mafi in Vaini when his Dad, Dr Kuli Helu, sent him on an errand to her one morning. 'Iteni was educated at Newington College, Sydney for a few years so he was quite new to family protocol at this stage. Mafi was attending to her family's breakfast. She was immaculately dressed. The kitchen was tidy and very clean. The children were seated with their meal all set out with their plates, cups and cutlery in front of them. 'Iteni commented that it was an unusual sight in Tonga at that time. Very little homes owned crockery or cutlery. He knew that most of Mafi's children attended THS. On this day, he noticed that 'Aleki and Mosiana were eating bread and drinking tea. When Mafi spoke, he thought she had a beautiful soft voice, similar to her sister 'Ana Mounga's voice. He described her sister Numia's voice as sharp or shrill and Meliana's as *fakaoloolo* (guarded).

Our house in Vaini was weatherboard and had a similar design to all the other *faifekau* homes but with the front and back verandas enclosed, unlike Ma'ufanga. This made the house feel bigger with the 2 extra enclosed areas. There was also a proper office. The front yard was completely fenced off. The back yard was open except for a small enclosure for some pigs. Mafi soon grew some vegetables beside the *peito*.

The kitchen was a biggish outhouse at the end of a 5m walkway from the house. The buildings were a metre above the ground. Then there was the usual *peito* with the fireplace for cooking at ground level.

Mafi's brother, Hanipale arrived from Foa to work our *'api uta* in Vaini to help our finances and his own family in Foa. This was very similar to his efforts while we were in Kolovai.

To help with the needs of the family, Pesi remembers taking Mafi's boiled puddings in custard sauce (*Polini Puteni*) to Nakao's shop on the main street of Vaini, to sell. The older the children got, the more the financial demand on our upkeep and education. Mafi decided to cut up her valuable *Kies* (special precious fine white mat) and tapa cloths to make purses, handbags, photo frames, fans, cushions etc which she sold at *Langa Fonua*. It wasn't always easy for Mafi to part with her koloa, especially the ones that her special aunt, 'Ana Mounga Feleti Goedicke, had bequeathed to her. Mafi explained to us girls that it was more important for her to provide for our educational needs and living then. In future, she said that her children would be able to buy themselves the koloa they needed provided they were well educated. Mafi was being prophetic and absolutely correct in her assessment of our situation then and now of course.

Koloa is the term for women's 'valuables' that are passed on from generation to generation. The most valuable koloa comprise of rare mats that can only be made in Samoa, Niuatoputapu or Niuafo'ou. 50

foot tapa cloths were also valuable. They could be cut up and used like blankets at night. As one piece, it is for show of wealth or position in society, especially if the 'kupesi' (art design patterns on it) was of special significance.

EDUCATION

Vaini is about the same distance by road to Nuku'alofa as Houma is. Transport loomed its head again for our parents. However, the eastern end of Tongatapu is much wider than the western end and therefore has more population. Hence there were more trucks and buses (by this time, buses were starting to be introduced as a means of people movers) running to and from Nuku'alofa. Lute and Mosiana were back at QSC Boarding School again. After our move, Mum and Dad decided to send Pesi and 'Aleki to board with Mafi's first cousin Palu Naulala. Thinking back now, this could have been to relieve Mum from her early morning routine as well as minimise cost of travel. Pesi was in Form 4 (Year 10) at THS, and 'Aleki was in Form 2 (Year 8). Monday to Friday routine at Palu and Nau's home was a big change for them.

Fig 46. Palu Naulala lived a very happy and long life here in Melbourne until she passed away at 91 years old, on 9th July, 2016.

It was quite an experience for 'Aleki and Pesi living away from home. However, it was less hassle for them and for Mum. Each morning they got dressed and had breakfast with the rest of the family. They walked back there for lunch which was always a *haka* (eg boiled vegetables and *luu lolo'i*). Nau grew a lot of young tapioca in their kitchen vegetable patch. Palu turned them into *'amio* tapioca (tapioca boiled in coconut cream till tender). Nau had a big *'api kolo* and *'api 'uta*. He used a bicycle to travel back and forth from his *'api 'uta*. 'Aleki and Pesi did their homework on the soft matted floor, used a kerosene lamp for light, and with the whole family surrounding them. Mele Toa'ila and 'Amalani had started at primary school but had no homework then. To sleep, Mele Toa'ila, 'Amalani and Pesi shared a king size bed that was curtained off on one end of the Tongan hut. Everyone else slept on rolled out beddings on the floor. This was the normal night arrangement at the time, for most families who had thatched huts. Palu loved gardening. She had a beautiful white rose garden at the front of their property.

Palu and Nau had five young children then: Mele Toa'ila(f), 'Amalani Tonga(f), 'Esalili Naulala (m, deceased), Fane Kite (f). Patea Fonua (f, Nuku'alofa), 'Etivina Lovo (f, Fiji), was born last. In 1974, we assisted Palu and Nau's eldest daughter, Mele Toa'ila, with her wedding to her Australian husband, John Ware, in Melbourne. Their second daughter, 'Amalani, followed to Melbourne later.

At THS, it was normal for the up-coming Form 5 (Lower Form 5) students to join the former Form 5s (Upper Form 5) in the same classroom to prepare for the NZ School Certificate Exam. THS students took this Certificate Exam in their Upper Form 5 year. However, early in Pesi's Lower Form 5 year, her senior teacher, Mr Jacobsen, announced that 3 students from this class were to attempt the NZ Certificate that year (1961). Sebastian Hurrell, Sione Liava'a and Pesi were the 3 students selected. Sebastian previously studied in Fiji so his command of English was excellent. Sione Liava'a and Pesi had been in the same class right from Form 1.

Meanwhile, Lute was not coping with boarding at QSC, unlike her first year there when she was travelling from Ma'ufanga daily. She liked studying at night but this was forbidden. Next, she attempted hiding under her bed with a lantern. For her trouble, she was caned by the tutor Kolotina Helu (Mum's niece). Apparently, Mosiana and cousin Soana Finau were furious with Kolotina and told her so. As expected, her exam marks tumbled. She asked Mum and Dad to let her come home the year after.

At the beginning of 1961, Lute, 'Aleki and Pesi all came home again to allow for Lute and Pesi to best prepare for their important exams (Maamaloa for Lute and NZ Certificate for Pesi). Dad's office was in great demand. Mr Beer from New Zealand, was the Principal of THS when we were at Vaini. He instigated a system of visiting the senior students' homes to check that they had suitable home study environment. Pesi wonders what he thought of many of the homes he visited? Many students lived in houses like Palu and Nau's, maybe smaller.

At THS, there were end of year school picnics. Pesi's favourite picnic sites were where they travelled to the surrounding islands of Tongatapu. They went on the Government barge from the Vuna wharf to one of these uninhabited islands. Most enjoyable. Every student would come with bags full of goodies. The students swam and ate all day long. Pesi would come home absolutely black from a day in the sea water and sun. Pesi remembers being late back with 'Aleki at the end of one such picnic. Mr Beer, the School Principal kindly took them home in his four wheel drive.

Fig. 47. Mele Toa'ila's wedding 7 Sept 1974.
l-r: Peter, William, Jean, John Ware, Mele Toa'ila,
Mosiana, Mele Vea, Pesi, Mapa Taloa. Front:
Siukimoana and Mafi Taumoepeau (later Weir).

HOME LIFE

As before, Mum was very involved in the Women's Association, Langa Fonua. She also belonged to the Ako 'Angelo (Combined Women's prayer group). Activities of these groups required that she travelled to Nuku'alofa often to attend meetings. These meetings must have given Mum a good opportunity to meet up with her school friends. She continued to teach bread making, cooking, cleanliness and housekeeping to adult women. She continued teaching the same skills at QSC at the request of Ms Rowlands, the Principal of QSC, and her friend Liu Tongilava, Head Tutor.

Panitita Helu Piutau (69 year's old), recalled in June 16, 2004

Panitita returned to Mafi and Sione's home in 1961. (Mafi and Sione looked after her and her brother as 5 and 4 year olds. Mafi was at the beginning of producing 2 launima (50 metre long) tapa cloths. This is arduous work. First the bark of the mulberry plants had to be stripped off the long thin stems and peeled the outer skin. Panitita's job was to drape these on a long wooden log and fakapaa 'a e tutū (beat until they had widened to double their widths). Mafi then would continue beating until their widths were 3 times wider again (known as "tutu"). The next steps required a lot of women sitting at opposite sides of a curved surface trestle. They would glue together the sheets of tapa cloth as well as imprint patterns on the cloths using kupesi (stencils). This process is continued until the resulting cloth was 10 feet wide and 50 feet long.

Afterwards the women would stretch the finished tapa cloth on the grass to dry out in the sun for a few days. The resulting cloths would then go through a process of highlighting the stencil patterns by painting around its edges with koka (black natural paints) over the curved surface trestle. Again the long tapa cloths needed to be thoroughly dried out in the sun.

Mafi next asked Panitita to go to Fahefa to her Aunty Vaimoana (Panitita's mum's sister) and ask her to help make some coconut body lotion ('*lolo*'). They made eight 1 litre bottles (ex-kerosene bottles) of body lotion. Mafi went with Panitita, loaded with one *launima* tapa cloth and 7 litres of coconut oil, to the Ma'ufanga wharf to send her off to Ha'apai to her father Hanipale and her brothers. Mum instructed Panitita when she got to Foa to cut up the huge tapa cloth into blanket sized pieces for her Dad and brothers. The coconut oil was to be re-bottled into smaller bottles for her family daily use. Her family was very grateful and happy with their gifts.

A typical weekday for Mafi in 1960 as Panitita observed, started at 4am. She would rise, put on a long black coat, wrap a scarf around her head and go outside to the peito. She would boil the big black kettle for the children's wash. A haka for the children's lunch would be ready by sunrise. She would get warm bath water ready in the bathroom, squeeze toothpaste onto the individual toothbrushes (to prevent wastage if the children did it themselves). There was always soap, body powder, body lotion, toothpaste available in Mafi's house.

Fig 48. Drying newly made tapa cloths.
Photo supplied by Helen R. Taliai.

What Panitita remembered most about 'Aleki was how gentle Mafi was with him. To wake him up in the morning, she was tentative. In a very soft voice, she would say,"'Alekisanita, please wake up (faka'a'a hake), please wake up it is day time now."

Panitita told a story about how Mafi would find some quick cash for Pesi's school requirements. Apparently after Pesi told Mafi about some 'kavenga' (requirement), Mafi told her it would be fine. As soon as Pesi left for school, Mafi pulled out a beautiful *kie tonga* (white fine mat), cut it up and made it into cushions. She took them to someone who paid her handsomely for them. Mafi often made similar artefacts and took them to the waterfront at Nuku'alofa to sell to tourists who arrived on Pacific Cruises. One time, Panitita recalled, a *palangi* couple(tourist) stopped to converse with Mafi. Mafi explained that the reason for her little venture was to increase the income of her family of 6 children and a Church Minister husband. The *palangis* bought all her wares, to Panitita's and Mafi's delight, allowing them to pack up early and travel back to Vaini.

Fig 49. Carrying out the process of tapa making.
Photos supplied by Helen R. Taliai.

Lute, at this stage, was into looking attractive. She loved to iron her clothes just before wearing them. Mafi's system for the family ironing was to do all of it on Saturday, fold them and put in each person's clothes box. Lute hated the Tongan custom of putting coconut oil on one's hair. Lute thought it was disgusting and dirty. She refused to put oil on her hair. Mosiana advised her that her hair will all fall out if she didn't do it. Lute loved to pull her waist band tight to accentuate her small waistline.

Panitita loved observing how Mafi dealt with her children if they were unhappy. An incident of how Mafi responded to Mele Si'i's tears when she was about 8 years old. Mele arrived from school crying uncontrollably. Mafi asked her calmly what had happened. Mele said a girl at school hit her. Mafi's method of stopping her cry was to distract her from her misery. She told her that she loved her and that she was happy because she knew Mele never cried for long. Mele soon stopped crying. Mafi asked if she was still sad. Mele said that she was but now she is not.

Mafi must have still worried about her brother's younger children. She took a short trip to Foa. She instructed Panitita in setting up her fireplace in her peito, like Mafi's in her home. Mafi explained to Panitita how she must teach her younger brothers, Lemeki and Fatai, to do 'feminine chores' like washing, ironing, make coconut oil, cook their food. Bottles must be cleaned using certain leaves. They were taught to help tidy their house as well. Lemeki and Fatai became excellent helpers to Panitita after Mafi left them for Tongatapu.

Mafi advised Panitita and Lesieli Palovitenisi Helu (Mateaki Helu's daughter) on how to live frugally and wisely. They must put aside clean beddings, crockery and cutlery, dish cloths, towels, table cloths etc, for visitors to Foa from Tongatapu, like teachers and Church Ministers. If they had 3 sheets for example, use only one for themselves and reserve 2 for visitors. Panitita said that even though her own mum 'Akanesi, died when her children were very young, they learnt a lot from their aunt Mafi.

Panitita repeatedly said that she never ever heard Dad nor Mum raise their voices at each other. When they left a town, they took its citizens' hearts with them.

FT3. Taufa Mafile'o Helu's Family Tree.

FAMILY TREE OF MAFI ANGAHIKI HELU'S MOTHER

Niua Mafile'o = Lehapi (Fakakai)
Potefela = Lepeka Ma'unofo'anga

Lisiate (M)

Siulolo

Mele Finau = Saia Malolo

- Kosi (m)
- Longatau (m)
- Su'e
  - Poise
  - 'Elisiva
  - Mele Vea
  - 'Okusi

Fane Semisi Mafileo = Siki Ma'unofo'anga
= Ma'ata (d of Hoke Fineanganofo)

Maile
'Ana Hala'ehi
Kolo
Vaipulu
Vili Fa'inga
Maani

'Ana Mo'unga = LatuPaa

Numia = Taloa

Mahe
Pinomi = Sala
Mapa
Tu'utanga = Pua
Taufa
Muli
Tu'utanga
Pouono
Feke'ila
Penisimani
'Isileli

Taufa Mafile'o = Sonatane Helu

Hanipale = 'Akanesi

Panitita
'Apataki Helu
Losipeli Helu V11
Mele Lahi
Lemeki Helu
Fatai Fuimaono Helu
Hopoate

Meliana = Mahe Finau

Sioana
Hanipale
Sikipio
Penisimani
Nanuma

Mafi Angahiki = Rev Sione F. Sisifa

Mosiana Francis
Lute Aleamotu'a
'Ilisapesi Weir
'Alekisanita Sisifa
Mele Sisifa
Dr Latu Sisifa

Tufui

Toakase 'Ana = Hosea (Fijian)

'Uiha Mafile'o = Mele Fale'aka (Faleloa)

Fahiva Vai

'Alipate Mele Fale'aka
Fe'ao
'Ilaise
Loata

Mele = Masiu

Palu
Mele T. Ware
'AmalaniTonga
'Esalili Naulala
Fane Kite
Etivina Lovo
Patea Fonua

Taufa Kesaia = Nau

Pauline Manu'atu
Dr Linda Manu'atu

'Ana Folau

Ma'ake Manu'atu

She related a very funny incident that happened in Vaini. Mafi and Sione were getting ready to attend a birthday party in the neighbourhood. Makasini and Sione Tauelangi's youngest daughter, Malini, was having her 1st birthday celebration. Dad always forgot the name Makasini (a relative of Mafi's). He asked Mafi to please remind him of her name (Makasini) during the party when he gave her the cue. On their return, Dad could not stop laughing. Apparently, every time Dad asked Mafi a question, she whispered 'Makasini'. So Dad was none the wiser with all his queries that evening.

Panitita's family after she got married

Panitita was asked by the Minister of Police, 'Akau'ola, at her New Year's feast where her name came from. She explained that her aunt Mafi Helu Sisifa named her after a well-to-do young woman in India, called Panitita Ramaby. She felt sorry for the millions of children who had no homes and lived on the streets. She built a huge home and set it up as an orphanage for many of the homeless children.

Panitita (f, Nuku'alofa dc) was the eldest of Hanipale and 'Akanesi's 9 children. The others were: Falanisi (m, Foa, dc), 'Apataki (m, North NZ, dc), Seini (f, Nuku'alofa), Losipeli Helu 6 (m, dc), Mele Lahi (f, Utah, dc), Lemeki (m, Auckland, dc), Fatai (m, Nuku'alofa), Viliami or Vili (m, USA). Some of Hanipale's grandchildren are now in Auckland, Sydney and Melbourne.

Hanipale and his family remained close to Mafi's family throughout his life.

Fig 50. Pesi receiving her THS Form 5 Academic Award in 1961.

PRIZE GIVING EVENTS: THS AND QSC

At the end of every school year, all three schools THS, QSC and Tupou College had their Prize Giving evening on the same date. The THS Prize Giving event was held at the Fasi Government Primary School Hall in the early evening, presided by the Crown Prince, Tungī. THS was his school. The combined QSC and Tupou College Prize Giving event took place straight after, at the grounds of the Wesleyan Church Primary School in Kolomotu'a. Queen Sālote presided over that huge gathering.

Fig 51. 'Aleki receiving his Form 1 Academic Award in 1961

In the evening of these occasions, Mosiana and Lute would head straight to their gathering area at Kolomotu'a, while the rest of the family would start at Fasi for the THS event. Pesi started receiving awards when she was 13 years old and in Form 3 (Year 9). In 1960 and 1961, she came top of her class. 'Aleki had been receiving Excellence Awards from the start of his years at THS. He topped many of his subjects each year. After receiving their THS awards, the family would rush over to Kolomotu'a to watch Mosiana receive her Awards (including Maamaloa in 1960). Lute received her top of class Awards ever since she joined QSC (including her Maamaloa and Loumaile in 1961). Mafi and Rev Sione must have been extremely proud of their children on these occasions.

CHAPTER 8

You must do the things you think you cannot do.
Eleanor Roosevelt

THE FAMILY UNIT BREAKS UP. 1962

The New Zealand School Certificate results were announced at the beginning of 1962. Pesi did well and she received an academic Australian Commonwealth Scholarship to study in Auckland. She remembers very well the excitement and apprehension at the time. Mum told Pesi that she was very happy that she was going overseas as it would give her great opportunities in the future. At that time, Mum was experiencing a lot of pain in her upper back, which must have been the sign of her cancer. She had a masseur come home once or twice to give her a massage on her back, but it did not help much.

Ask and it will be given to you. Matthew 7:7.
A story by Lute and Viliami

As our family needed extra money for the three lots of school fees, transport, and to prepare for Pesi's trip to New Zealand, Mum and Dad, as usual, tried to find ways to resolve their financial challenges. Dad decided to go and ask Her Majesty, Queen Sālote, to allow him to collect coconuts that fell outside the fence of her Kauvai Estate, to turn into copra. The Kauvai Estate is within the Vaini Church District. Mafi did not approve of this idea. Nevertheless, Dad resolved to give it a go. Dad spent a day at the Palace. On the second day, HM Queen Sālote asked her lady-in-waiting/nurse, Susana Helu, (Siosaia Fatai Helu's daughter), "Why do I see the Faifekau outside? Please go and ask him what he wants." Susana took Dad in. HM Queen

Sālote told him to return home, she would organise for Manu Kauvai (the caretaker of Kauvai Estate) to drop a load of coconuts off at his place later. After two weeks, a big truck from the Kauvai Estate pulled up outside the parsonage to drop off about 23 sacks of ready-made copra. This was far beyond Dad's imagination. It gave Mafi and Sione enough cash to finance the family for the coming school year.

This is but one instance of how HM Queen Sālote Tupou III earned her reputation as a ruler who possessed charm, intelligence, authority, knowledge of her people and was very kind to her people. She was also known to be scathing of those who did not carry out duty or where moral character was dubious. When she was described as possessing 'great mana', Queen Sālote commented, 'Yes, with intelligent manipulation.' *(historyofroyalwomen.com/tonga/queens-regnant-salote-tupou-iii)*

Pesi writes

To prepare for her big adventure, Mafi bought pieces of material to make her some clothes. Dr Kuli Helu's wife, 'Ana, was an excellent dressmaker. She made Pesi a dressing gown and two or three outfits.

On the day of her flight, Mum's eldest sister, Numia, her son Pinomi and 'Amalani Naulala were among those who went with them on a truck (still the main mode of transport) to the airport to see Pesi off. Little did Pesi know that that would be the last time she would see her Mum.

Students that were awarded scholarships in Auckland that year

From the Upper Fifth class
Academic course:
Litia Makakaufaki, Tualau Mangisi, Uasi 'Aholelei.
Ardmore Teacher Training College:
Latu Tupou, Saane Tufui.
Other: Mosese Fakatou.

From Lower Fifth class
Academic Course:
'Ilisapesi Sisifa, Sebastian Hurrell

Pushing the boundaries of freedom in Vaini.

One day after school, a Vaini girlfriend and neighbour of ours, Nusi Makahununui asked Lute to follow her. Nusi wanted to accompany the Captain of a Cruise ship that was in the harbour that day before she and Lute headed back to Vaini. Lute agreed to follow Nusi. In the meantime, Mum and Dad were worried sick for Lute's safety. When she finally turned up late, she was told off and lectured about her folly.

Mosiana's First Ball

At the beginning of 1962, Mosiana started at the Teacher Training College in Nuku'alofa. She was aware that her *palangi* lecturer, Mr Gower, favoured her in his classes. He blushed when talking to her. One day she was summoned to his office. He wanted to ask her to the Hospital Ball to be held at the *'Apimataka* (Copra Board Park). Mosiana told him that she needed to ask permission from her parents. When she asked Mum and Dad, Dad was happy with the idea while Mum was worried about people judging their decision. It was a difficult call to make, as Tonga was a very conservative society. Marriage to a *palangi* male was rare at that time. The idea that the daughter of the Faifekau would be seen around in a car with a *palangi*, was too much for Mum to contemplate. Dad tried to explain that this *palangi* was a trustworthy individual who was the Principal of the Teacher Training College. Their daughter was 19 and old enough to be taken out.

Fig 52. Mum and Dad at Fua'amotu Airport in January 1962, farewelling Pesi. Pinomi Taloa is at the back (on the truck).

Finally, Mosiana was allowed to go to the Ball. Mr Gower offered to pay for her ball gown. Mum and Mosiana chose white organza material. Dr Kuli Helu's wife, 'Ana, was again the dressmaker. She made a beautiful gown of white lace that had a small waist with a full flared skirt. On the eve of the Ball, Mr Gower arrived in his car. Mum insisted that 'Aleki (who was 13 years old then) accompany the couple to the Ball. Mum was left to have a sleepless night. As they started out, Mr Gower asked Mosiana for the meaning of her little brother going with them. Mosiana told him that it was Tongan custom to have a relative to accompany a girl on her dates.

Mr Gower asked again to take Mosiana to a skating competition at Lapaha. Dad approved and they went. At this time, Na'a Fiefia was the Vice Principal at the Teachers College. Na'a asked a student colleague of Mosiana's, Veiongo Mafi to pass on to Mosiana that she should not go out with Mr Gower. That killed that friendship immediately. Dad then explained to Mosiana that he preferred his daughters to marry overseas people. Life would be easier with them than with Tongans. There won't be cooking in an open fireplace outside, your homes would be all set-up so that all chores will be inside the house. Mosiana admitted to her sister Lute, that these words made a strong impression on her mind from then on and influenced her choice of a husband when the time came.

Family connection with Na'a Fiefia later continued in Hawaii, Tonga and then in Melbourne. Na'a's daughter, Kilisitina, married youngest Sisifa son, Dr Sione Latu Sisifa.

Lute's perspective

After Pesi left for New Zealand in January 1962, Mafi took a short trip to Ha'apai to check on her brother Hanipale and his children (described by Panitita Helu in her interview). On Mafi's return from Foa, she was experiencing much more pain than when she confided in Pesi before she left for Auckland. According to Mosiana and Lute, Mum checked into the old Vaiola Hospital and asked them to admit her to the Tuberculosis Ward. She suspected that the great pain in her back and chest were caused by TB.

Doctors 'Alo 'Eva, Posesi Fanua, Kuli Helu, Tilitili Puloka and 'Opeti Lutui were all working at Vaiola Hospital at this time. After examining Mum, they told her that she was suffering from cancer not TB. So Mafi was admitted to a General Ward. This ward had double rows of beds and an aisle down the middle. There were two enclosed verandas on either side with a single row of beds each. Mosiana was asked to help look after our Mum while she was in hospital. Mosiana slept under Mafi's bed. Every morning, Mosiana gave Mafi her breakfast before she went to school. The hospital was next door to QSC. Mosiana said that Mum was a most considerate and calm patient. Relatives and friends visited with food and came to pray and talk with her during the day. Mafi's sister Numia had a restaurant in town and so her family brought in Mafi's meals. Mosiana also said that in the evening, Mafi would walk down the aisle in the ward, read out a hymn, start singing, the patients would join in, then she would pray for them.

Lute and 'Aleki at this stage, stayed with aunt Palu Naulala in Kolomotu'a during the week, to attend THS and QSC. Dad looked after Mele and Latu at home in Vaini. Sister Mele explained that one day, Dad put both her and brother Latu on his bicycle. Mele sat on the front bar, and Latu was balanced on the back of the bicycle. They first went to a wharf on the foreshore of Nuku'alofa to see the RNZAF flying boat that rescued the people from Minerva Reef. They then continued to Vaiola Hospital to see Mum. The story of this shipwreck and its survivors dominated the local news during this time.

THE STORY OF THE SHIPWRECK

Documented by Olaf Ruhen in 'Minerva Reef'

On July 1962, a boat called 'Tuaikaepau' (slow but sure) with 17 men, left Nuku'alofa for Gisborne, NZ. The boat hit hard the edge of Telekitonga (Southern atoll) and sank. They saw a wrecked Japanese fishing boat nearby in the morning. They made this their home for the next 14 weeks as it was the only thing above the water in high tide. They waited in vain for rescue. Their families all believed they had died and held funeral services for them.

Fig 53. Japanese boat marooned at a M. reef.

Fig 54. A flagstaff on one M. reef.

Their daily routine included prayers first thing in the morning. They were rostered to carry out necessary duties. They collected rain water and distilled pure water from sea water to drink. They fished every day for food.

After a few weeks (end of August), Captain Tevita Fifita decided to start building an outrigger canoe with which to seek help. They used tools found on the Japanese boat and material from both wreckages. Tevita, his son, and a crew member set out northwards to try to reach Fiji. They arrived at Kadavu Island and had to abandon their canoe and swim over the reef to land. After some time in the water, Tevita's son said that he could no longer swim. They held each other and prayed before letting go of him. He drowned.

On Monday 16th October, a RNZAF Sunderland flying boat dropped off supplies at Minerva Reef. On Tuesday 17th October, it picked up 10 crew members and 1 body and took them to the Colonial War Memorial Hospital in Suva. They were dehydrated and under-nourished. One showed signs of TB, and 5 were bedridden.

They were flown back to Nuku'alofa and taken to Vaiola Hospital where they remained until they were fit enough to go home.

These days, the two Minerva Reefs are very popular. About 400 yachts visit or pass close by so the Tuaikaepau could have been rescued much more quickly if that was the case in 1962.

Later on, Tonga declared ownership of the Reefs. The Tongan Government sent the Honourable Minister of Police, 'Akau'ola, Inspector of Police, Siaosi Maeakafa Aleamotu'a (Lute's husband), some police force members and some prisoners (as workers) to the Minerva Reefs. They erected 2 flag poles on the reefs.

Siaosi Maeakafa Aleamotu'a was given the honour of raising the flags as he was the grandson of Ma'afu'otu'itonga Aleamotu'a of the Lau Group. Maeakafa's mother, Sālote, was the daughter of Siaosi Maeakafa (Lute's husband's namesake). That Siaosi Maeakafa's parents were Tangakina Nuku and Sione Ngu (son of Tevita 'Unga, son of Tupou I).

MUM'S LAST MONTHS

Dr 'Alo 'Eva performed Mafi's previous major operation when the family was in Kolovai. Dr Posesi Fanua was Dad's cousin from Lofanga. Dr Kuli Helu was Mafi's first cousin. Dr Tilitili Puloka was from the Puloka family that brought up Mafi's dad, Sonatane Helu. Dr 'Opeti Lutui was the Dr in Niuatoputapu who brought doves home for our Sunday dinners and who delivered our sister Mele.

When the doctors could not help Mum any more, her cousin Dr Kuli Helu decided to take her to his home in Kolofo'ou so he could attend to her comfort and medical needs. He wanted to vacate a room for her in his house. Mafi asked that they build her a little outhouse in their backyard instead. Her male relatives gathered and built her a little hut outside Dr Kuli's home. Her sisters Numia, 'Ana Mo'unga, Meliana and first cousin, Neomai Helu Taliai, all took turns to look after her. She asked Dad to please not bring the children as they were distressed seeing her sick and it made her very sad. Dad visited her as often as he could. Her best friends, especially Sela Puloka, also visited her a lot to pray with her.

Mum passed away peacefully in November 1962. Ma'afu, Noble of Vaini, granted a well-positioned burial ground in his cemetery in the middle of Vaini for Mafi. Noble Ma'afu at this time was the brother of Lady Tuputupu, mother of the current Queen of Tonga, Queen Nanasipau'u.

Mafi was returned to Vaini that evening for her 'apoo (wake). Women were sent from the Palace with beautiful *'teu'* (mats and tapa cloths) to use for Mum's bed and room decoration. Very many people turned up from Mum's school days, work days, as well as relatives, and connections. The local primary school where sister Mele and brother Latu attended, marched to the graveyard. Miss Rowlands, the Principal of QSC, Miss Liu Tongilava, and QSC students also lined the Vaini main street leading to the cemetery for Mum's procession. The President of the Weslyan Church, Dr'Amanaki Havea led 12 Faifekaus in conducting Mafi Helu Sisifa's funeral. Mafi and Sione Sisifa's children still feel very honoured and amazed at the love and appreciation showed by all who attended and contributed to Mafi's farewell.

> *"When you were born you cried and everyone around you rejoiced. Live your life in a way that when you die, everyone around you will cry and you will rejoice."*
> *An old Indian Proverb.*

Perfect submission, perfect delight,	Taha 'ae 'ofa, taha e me'a!
Visions of rapture burst on my sight;	Kuo te hoko ko hono 'Ea:
Angels descending, bring from above	'Ea moe 'Alo ne ne pekia
Echoes of mercy, whispers of love.	Si'ono foha kuo ohia.
This is my story, this is my song,	Hoku monuu ee, eku koloa,
Praising my Saviour all the day long	'Ete ongo'I he taimi kotoa
This is my story this is my song,	Fakamo'oni fakapapau
Praising my Saviour all the day long.	Fale 'ae 'Eiki 'ia teau.

Free Wesleyan Hymn Book **(fwhb),** Tongan Hymn 610, Verse 2.
Author: Frances Jane Van Alstyne 1820-1915. Translated by Dr J.E.Moulton. Ref: *'E keu 'elelo afe mai!* Page 136, by Siupeli T. Taliai

DEVASTATION AFTER THE BURIAL

Lute cannot describe the absolute desolation she and everyone in the family felt returning home. Mum was gone. She would not hear her soft voice ever again. Gone were the days where, if Mafi was not at home after school, the children would hang around the doors and windows watching out for her arrival. Otherwise, she would be at home, busy with the never-ending household duties. Aunty Numia came and stayed for a few days. She took the children to Mum's *mala'e* or *fa'itoka* (burial ground) every evening.

Mosiana became the mother figure for sister Mele and baby brother Latu. Mosiana remembers hurrying home from her teaching job at QSC to find these two sitting patiently on the side steps, waiting for her. Pesi remembers that scene well in 1961 when she got home from THS at the end of the day, if Mafi was not yet home from a meeting.

Dad did the letter writing to Pesi in Auckland right from the beginning of 1962. He never mentioned that Mum was desperately ill. It was so devastating when someone's indiscretion in 'Atalanga led me to the discovery of Mum's passing. Devastation. Unbelievable. Desolation. How could that be? Pesi couldn't leave her little room for two or three weeks.

Epsom Girls Grammar was now on holidays. Pesi was most miserable. She did not have to sit the University Entrance Exam because her internal results were above the required standard. Dad must have been struggling with how best to tell her about Mum's terminal illness. Mafi was in good hands with her relatives and friends. Dad however had his job and all of the children to worry about.

Dad's faith saw him through this most difficult time. According to Lute and Mosiana, Dad's Vaini congregation and relatives were most supportive of Dad and his children for the rest of their time in Vaini.

Fig 55. Outside our home in Vaini (sideview), Dec 1962.
l-r: Lute, Latu, Numia, Mele, Mosiana, 'Aleki.

Fig 56. Members of the Vaini Church choir with their Award. 1962.

Holaki Helu (Dr Kuli's son) was at Auckland in 1962 on a scholarship. He was visiting Tonga at the time of Mum's funeral. He took the following photos.

DAD'S STRUGGLES

Teenager Lute's last fling, December 1962

School broke up for the Christmas holidays in December 1962. Lute's girl friends in Vaini asked her to go with them to a dance in the local community hall close to home. She went without asking for Dad's permission. While they were on the dance floor, she caught a glimpse of Dad outside the hall. Maybe someone went and alerted him. Dad came inside, grabbed her hand and took her home. He told her not to go out dancing in public like that ever again. It was not acceptable especially with his position in the church. Lute knew Dad really meant what he said. She knew Dad was most disappointed in her. He then asked aunt Numia to speak to Lute. Numia gave Lute a stern talking to. Numia explained that Lute should not keep local boy friends. Lute needed to be more discerning in her choice of friends, especially with a view to her future. It may have been acceptable for her, Numia, to marry a Vaini local but Lute should be thinking more of a boyfriend in Nuku'alofa. Lute took this advice to heart. She explained that this anecdote ended any desire of hers to 'look sideways' at any boys in Vaini. 'Spare the rod and spoil the child.'

Fig 57. l-r: Latu, Mosiana, Dad, Lute, 'Aleki, Mele with the choir's Cup.

At the beginning of 1963, Miss Dilys Rowlands granted Lute a scholarship to attend Form 7 at the newly formed Tupou High School in Fasi (THSF). Miss Rowlands explained to Dad and Lute that she would give Lute a scholarship to study overseas after THSF. This THSF was newly formed for post Maamaloa and Loumaile students from QSC and Tupou College. They were selected from the top students of the 2 colleges. This new school was held in the Royal waiting room at Saione Fo'ou. Some of Lute's classmates were: Kalapoli Paongo, Tevita Afeaki, Kilifi Heimuli and Pita Niuvao.

In July 1963, Dad, Mosiana, Lute, 'Alekisanita, Mele and Latu moved to Fasi (in Nuku'alofa) without Mum. Pesi was in Auckland. Cousin Viliami Sisifa came back and joined the family again there. As it turned out, this posting was to be Sione Finau Sisifa's last. The older children were old enough to make considered decisions of their own destinies. Dad and Mum's caring and deliberate nurturing of their children were about to be manifested in their own choices.

Fig 58. MUM'S HEADSTONE AT VAINI, 2017.
l-r: Argosy Aleamotu'a; Viliami (Papa), Pesi Lina Sisifa, Sione F. Sisifa and Jared 'Aleki Sisifa; …, Hanipale Finau, Pesi Taloa, …

Fig 59. 'Ana and Kuli Helu, at their daughter Mele's wedding.

Fig 60. 'Atalanga students 1963.
back row l-r: 'Aneti Vi, Wailangilala Tufui, Konai Helu, Pesi Sisifa, Saane Tufui.
middle row: Lu'isa Folaumoetu'i, 'Eseta Fulivai, Lita Taumoepeau, Kalolaine Taumoepeau, Litia Makakaufaki.
front row: Lavinia Faletau, Hola Fotu, Leafa Tuita, Latu Tupou.

FT4. Haveahikule'o's Descendents (Helu 1)

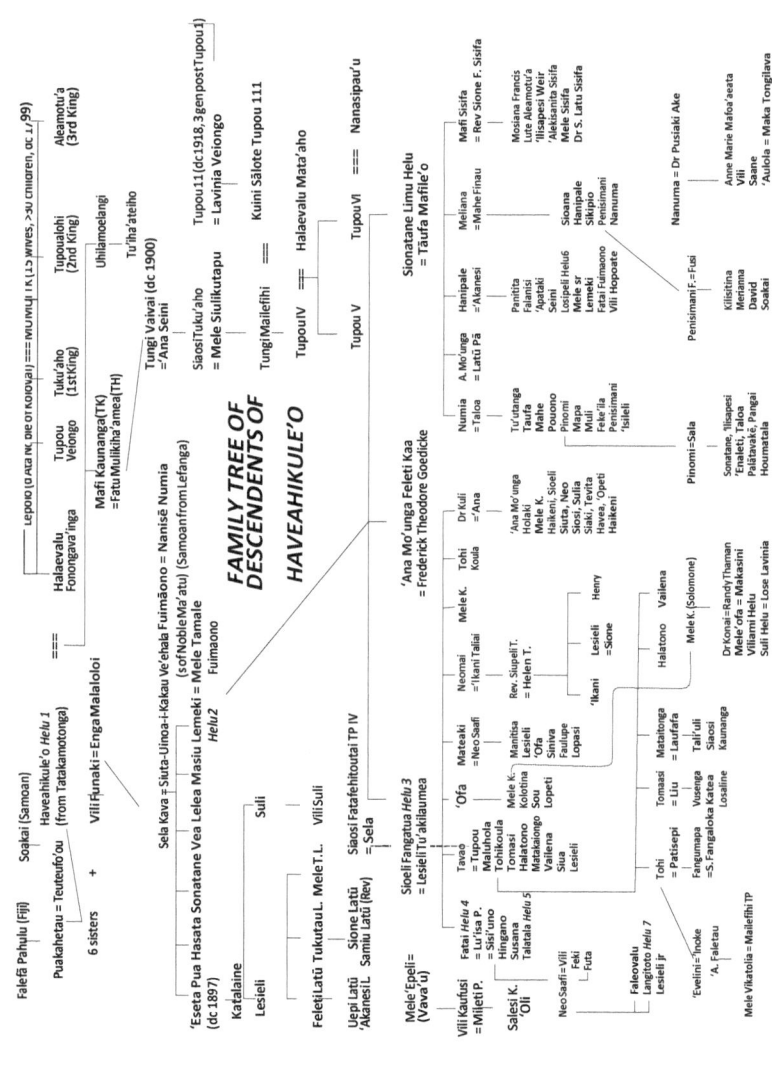

CHAPTER 9

Happiness resides not in possessions, not in gold, Happiness dwells in the soul.
Democritus.

FASI-MOE-AFI 1963–1965

Lute recalls how keenly she and Mosiana felt the love and welcome that the people of Fasi gave them when they arrived at this destination. They witnessed for the first time the sort of welcome the people of a 'new congregation' accorded to their new pastor. With all the moves before, the children would be exploring the new environment with no thoughts about food, where to sleep, preparation of meals and so on. This time, Mosiana and Lute sat with Dad to receive the food brought by the local people for the family. The girls got themselves reoriented to settle into their new home.

The *'api faifekau* in Fasi had similar layout to that in Vaini. The verandas were enclosed. The back one had 2 rooms partitioned off. 'Aleki used one room. Cousin Viliami Sisifa used the other one. Later, cousin Saimone Helu (Magistrate Hingano's eldest son) came to share 'Aleki's room so they could study together. Dad and Latu used the main bedroom on the right and the girls used the other main bedroom. At the front was a good sized office for Dad. The remaining section of the front enclosed veranda and the formal sitting room were used for receiving guests and visitors.

The girls, Mosiana and Lute, were by now moving in circles where some people had second hand chairs in their sitting rooms. After a while, the girls decided to knock together some chairs for the main sitting room.

As Mosiana was working as a teacher (or tutor as they were called) at QSC, she was sent girls who were on detention for various misdemeanors. Misdemeanors included: lateness to class or any designated event (like meals, prayer meetings, choir practice) and many others. The chores given them included: cooking, washing, ironing, sweeping the grounds, cleaning the house, and errands. As well, Mafi Hingano, Saimone Helu's mother sent her sister Finau every Saturday to go and help with washing clothes.

Cousin Viliami had attended Tupou College but did not enjoy the experience much. He skipped classes often. Dad's blood pressure was still not 'controlled' after his major stroke in Vaini. Viliami was asked to go and help out with some housework and other physical duties that Dad could not perform. Viliami was a godsend to the family at this time.

Mosiana and Lute made some good friends with the neighbours. Among them were: Tu'ifua Vuna, Pauline Vuna (married to cousin Futa Helu at the time) and 2 other sisters; Vaimoana 'Aholelei Pahulu and husband Kioa Pahulu; Bishop Halapua and children Lesieli, Sione and Meleane.

MOSIANA'S CAREER IN TONGA

At the end of Mosiana's 6 months Teacher Training Course, the Tongan Government gave the graduates a Pacific Tour (by boat) to Niue, American Samoa, Western Samoa and Suva (Fiji). It was a highlight of her life then for Mosiana, opening her eyes to the beauty of other Pacific islands, as well as that of the western cultures as seen in the 2 Samoas and Suva.

Mosiana then taught at QSC for a while. She was offered a Government Scholarship to study at Ardmore Teacher Training College in New Zealand. (Ardmore Teacher College was where ex-THS students were trained in 1962: Saane Tufui, Latu Tupou and Aneti Vi. The QSC Principal, Miss D. Rowlands, objected and refused to allow Mosiana to avail herself of this opportunity. Dad, asked The President of the Church, Rev Harris for help. Rev

Harris found a way to sidestep Miss D. Rowland's objection. He got a substitute scholarship for a 6 month's Teacher Training course in Hawaii instead. In Hawaii, Mosiana spent a lot of time with Na'a Fiefia, his wife 'Iunisi and very young daughter Kilisitina. Na'a Fiefia was on study leave in Hawaii at the time.

On Mosiana's return to Tonga, Miss D. Rowlands refused to give Mosiana back her teaching position at QSC. Dad appealed to Rev Harris again for help. Rev Harris found a Government position for Mosiana as a typist for the Honourable Minister of Lands, Noble Tuita.

At about this time, Mosiana was introduced to a palangi teacher from Victoria, Australia, Mr Bryan Francis. He was on a holiday and was staying with Dr Posesi Fanua's family. Lute had an inkling that Mosiana may in time marry this palangi.

Fig 61. Middle 2nd row l-r: teachers Mosiana Sisifa, Soana Havea, cousin Sioana Finau with QSC students.

Fig 62. Mosiana Sisifa, 1963.

PESI'S SHORT VISIT FROM AUCKLAND, JANUARY 1965

Litia Makakaufaki and Pesi worked as ward cleaners at the Cornwall Aged Care Hospital (now Bupa Cornwall Care Home) in Auckland during the school holidays of 1962 and 1963. They actually used a machine to polish the timber floors of the wards. They sent their pay back to their families in Tonga. Pesi took 2 weeks off to visit Dad and her family in Fasi at the end of January 1965. Pesi was 18 years old.

It was good to see everyone but she sorely missed seeing Mum at home. Dad's gait at this stage was hesitant and slow. Being young and inexperienced, Pesi did not know that medically, Dad's high blood pressure could be minimised. Pesi didn't find out how she could have helped him at this stage and assumed somehow he got the best and most appropriate medical help. 34 years later, Pesi suffered from hypertension (high blood pressure) in Australia, she then saw the very wide variety of medication that can be combined in various quantities to minimise its devastating effects on our bodily systems as we get older. Preventative measures can also be used effectively. Most of the Sisifa siblings now have high blood pressure starting at around age fifties. The youngest sibling, Dr Sione Latu Sisifa, regularly checks up on the rest of the siblings to make sure they follow good preventative lifestyles to minimise the effect of their disease.

Pesi saw how the family dynamics were altered without our Mum's presence. Mosiana and Lute took her under their wings. Pesi watched Latu trailing Dad instead of 'Aleki following Dad around at that age. Mele watched Mosiana every minute when she was home from work. Pesi observed Dad's quiet influence, but mostly, Mosiana and Lute were making decisions regarding themselves and the household. Pesi was touched seeing cousin Viliami performing some of the chores that resulted from Mum's absence. Thinking back, Viliami was only in his late teens. He was with the family again but in a very different capacity.

Many family members visited: Dr Kuli Helu and wife 'Ana, Professor Futa Helu's mother Sisi'uno Helu, Magistrate Hingano Helu and wife Mafi. The children visited some relatives including Numia, Taloa and family.

Fig 63. Sisi'uno Helu, Futa's mother, at the Fasi parsonage, Jan 1965.

Fig 64. Mafi Hingano and Magistrate Hingano Helu seeing Pesi off at the airport, 1965.

Fig 65. 'Ana and Dr Kuli Helu at the airport 1965.

Fig 66. Farewelling Pesi at Fua'amotu Airport, Jan 1965.
back row l-r: 'Aleki, Muni (Tevita), Viliami.
2nd row: Lute, Dad, Pesi, Mosiana front row: Latu, Mele. in the background: aunties Neomai Taliai, Numia Taloa.

DEVELOPMENT OF LUTE'S CAREER. JULY 1964

Lute was aware that Dad's health was deteriorating. She noticed that his movement was slow and his speech was slurred. She began to worry about where Dad and his family would retire to in the event of his health failing him. She hatched a plan and acted on it immediately. She had completed 6 months at Tupou High School. She spoke to Dad about her plan. She saw Miss Rowlands and apologised to her for not finishing her course. She explained that with Dad's failing health, she needed to start work and support him and the family. She immediately got a job at 'Oto Sanft's business as financial manager. Meanwhile, she also was looking for a Government job. She sat a typing test which was administered by Tangoi Folaumoetu'i at the Premier's Department. Lute got the job as the receptionist for Hon. Minister of Police, Manoa Havea.

Fig 67. Lute started work, 1963.

She was thrilled. The pay was very good when compared to the 4 sovaleni per month Mosiana got from the church during and after she attended the Teacher Training College. 1 Sovaleni was equivalent to a British £1 (the Tongan currency at the time).

Church ministers who were from other islands and therefore did not own 'apikolo in Tongatapu, asked the nobles where they worked for land in preparation for their retirement. Unfortunately, Mum and Dad had not considered this eventuality as they were only in their 40s when they were in Vaini.

Lute decided that the solution to her dilemma was to marry someone who owned an 'api kolo in Kolomotu'a. She asked her friends and neighbours at the time, Moana and Kioa Pahulu, for names that fitted her criteria. They named 2 prospects, Maeakafa Fielakepa Aleamotu'a was one of them. Lute mulled this over and decided that Maeakafa Fielakepa was her preference.

Fig 68. Newly weds Maeakafa and Lute, 1965

She had seen Maeakafa around but she didn't know him well. He was a policeman and was stationed at Mu'a at the time. The Hospital

Ball was coming soon. She saw Maeakafa when he came to her office to collect his pay at the end of the month. She approached him to see if he would like to partner her to the Hospital Ball. He accepted. For the next few weeks they spoke often in the lead-up to the Ball. Lute also found a Ball partner for Mosiana, Tu'amelie Fusimalohi.

The two girls found beautiful used ball gowns from Mate Lemoto's clothes shop (at his Shipping Company Store). Mosiana chose a blue waisted long frock and Lute picked a green frock of the same style. They dieted for the occasion. They felt like princesses on the eve of the Ball. The boys arrived in a car to take them to the Ball. Lute described her elation at dancing with her 'prince'. She thought he was the best looking there.

Even though there were other boys that visited her at home at the time, Maeakafa stood out for her.

Fig 69. Lute at the Nuku'alofa Market, 1965.

Lute was very impressed that he always dressed well, always wore a ta'ovala (waist mat) when visiting her and was very respectful of her and her family. Lute became aware then that Maeakafa's father was the Noble of Kolomotu'a but she did not know that in actual fact, the Aleamotu'a family was the Landed Aristocrats of Kolomotu'a.

Courting girls in Tonga in the 1960s involved the males visiting the girl's home accompanied by a small party of their male friends and relatives. Sometimes, they would ask permission to hold a kava party at the girl's house. The girl then would prepare the kava for the males to drink.

LUTE'S MAJOR DECISION ON HER FUTURE

After four weeks of Maeakafa visiting Lute, she asked him if he was actually serious about a future with her or whether he was just whiling time away. Maeakafa asked her to qualify her question. She told him that if he had no intention of marrying her then please allow her to find someone who is more serious. Maeakafa replied, 'When you want to get married, we can go ahead and do it.'

They then planned their wedding

Without a word to Maeakafa's family nor to Lute's, at lunchtime of the next day, Lute made her way to the Marriage Registration office. Maeakafa was waiting there with Afui Kalaniuvalu. They got their Marriage Certificate. The boys left and Lute continued on to the Magistrate Office to see her uncle, Magistrate Hingano Helu. She told him about her Marriage Certificate, he asked to whom was she marrying. When she told him Maeakafa, he gave her his seal of approval. After work, she went around to Hingano's office again. Lute saw Maeakafa waiting in a car under the casuarina tree by the market place. Hingano and Lute picked him up and they went to the town of Pea to Rev Tonga Simiki's *'api Faifekau*. Rev Tonga Simiki conducted their wedding. (Rev Tonga Simiki was Dad's mum's second cousin.)

Magistrate Hingano drove them back to Nuku'alofa where they parted, each of them going home alone.

That evening, Maeakafa's uncle, Tiuke Aleamotu'a, and some of Maeakafa's family, arrived at Dad's house to announce that Maeakafa and Lute were married and that they were there to take her to his home. They took her to Tiuke's house where Maeakafa's dad, Noble

Saia Fielakepa presided over a Kava party. At nightfall, Lute and Maekafa went to Maeakafa's family home next door to Tiuke's house.

LUTE'S FUTURE HOME

Like all newly-weds in Tonga at the time, Lute and Maeakafa lived with Maeakafa's parents with younger brothers and two sisters under the same roof. Saia Aleamotu'a was very unwell.

Tu'i Kanokupolu V was King Aleamotu'a, one of Tu'i Kanokupolu Mumui's sons. Lute's father-in-law, Noble Saia Aleamotu'a, owned a huge family compound in the middle of Kolomotu'a. Noble Ata's family (aristocrats of Kolovai) had the use of a corner section of this family compound at the time Lute and Maeakafa got married.

Before Noble Saia Aleamotu'a passed away, he asked Noble Ata to vacate the corner block of land in his family compound so that Maekafa and Lute could move in there. Both Lute and Maekafa had only just started at their jobs and had no savings to build a house on their block of land. Their pays were only enough to help with the family daily needs.

DAD RETIRES

Dad's health had deteriorated to a stage that he could not continue with his job. He retired and moved to the home of his second cousin Taulanga Nonu's home in Kolofo'ou. Taulanga was married to a Kolomotu'a woman, Nasaleti Pahulu (sister of Kioa Pahulu) FT5. Uncle Hingano Helu stepped in and took 'Aleki to his home to continue studying with his son Saimone.

Soon Mosiana found that she did not get on with Nasaleti. Dad approached Rev Harris for his pension to help build a small house for himself. Mosiana asked Mafi's first cousin Tufui if Dad could build a small house on his large block of land in Kolofo'ou. Tufui did not have a family of his own so he was happy to welcome Dad there. Mosiana mobilised uncle Hanipale Helu to build Dad a timber house at Tufui's place. Professor Futa Helu and his wife, Pauline, provided labour from their University/Tafe called 'Atenisi.

Mosiana moved Dad, sister Mele, brother Latu, and Mele Lahi into this house before she left for Hawaii on her Teacher Training Scholarship. Mele Lahi (Hanipale's daughter) moved in with them so she could help with housekeeping. They did not stay there long.

Mosiana had met an Australian teacher, Bryan Francis, while the family were still at Fasi. Not long after Mosiana's return from Hawaii, she and Bryan decided to get married. Dad was very pleased at the match as he knew that life in Australia would be much more preferable to what was available in Tonga then. Mosiana got engaged and married Bryan Francis on 14th May 1966 in Rosebud, Victoria.

Fig 70. Futa Helu during the time he was building up 'Atenisi University.

Maeakafa's eldest sister, Kaifonua Aleamotu'a was in Melbourne studying nursing at the time. She was bridesmaid at Mosiana's wedding. The rest of Mosiana's QSC school friends who were in Melbourne, attended the wedding as well.

Back in Tonga, Lute and Maeakafa decided to use part of Dad's pension to start building a cement house on their block of land. They borrowed the rest. Dad's timber house was moved into Lute and Maeakafa's block before their house construction started. Lute explained that it was a very difficult time for them all.

Fig 71. Bryan and Mosiana's wedding in Rosebud, 1965 with bridesmaid Kaifonua Aleamotuʻa and best man Dr Paul Francis.

Lute was flat out with her full time Government job. She had her husband, two young ones, Argosy Brittania and Mele Moala, Dad, sister Mele and brother Latu to care for. Maeakafa's mother, Salote, babysat her children during working hours and she provided lunch for Dad, Mele and Latu as well. Mele Lahi (or Mele Helu Sisifa) joined the family here again to help with the housekeeping and to relieve Sālote of some of the chores.

Lute and Maeakafa stepped up and filled the gap of caring for Dad when he needed us most. The rest of us siblings, can only thank them sincerely. Mum and Dad did their utmost to give their children the best life they could. Their children, are who they are today because of the special brand of nurturing and upbringing they planned and adopted for their children.

FT5. Rev Sione F. Sisifa's Ha'afeva Connections.

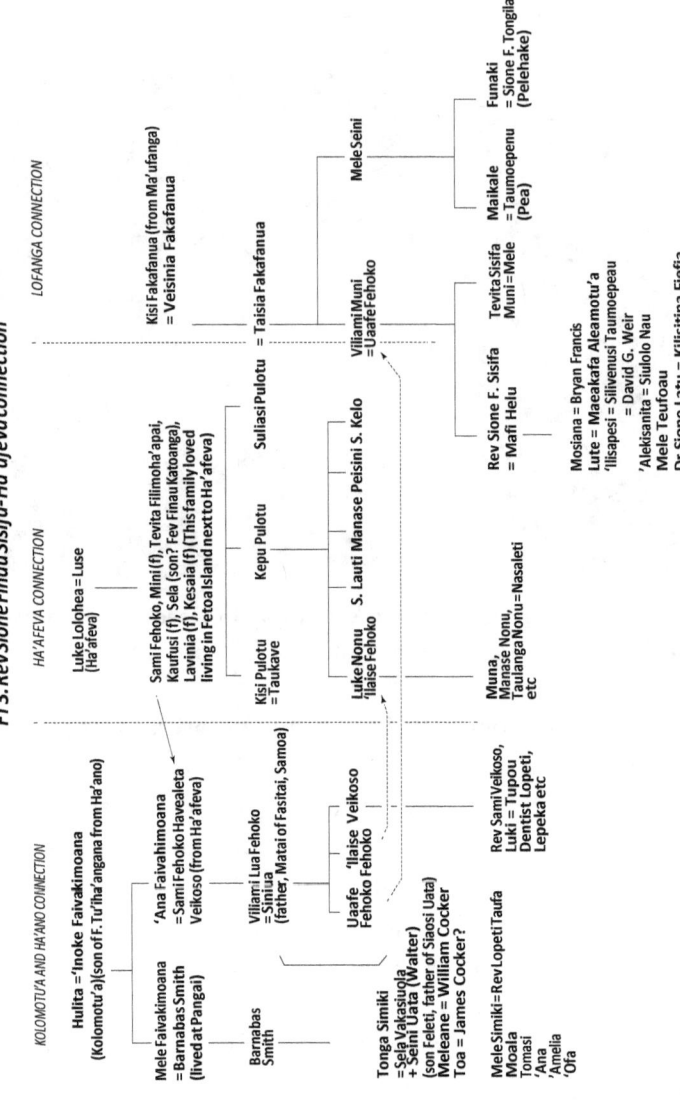

Fig 72. Inspector Siaosi Maeakafa Aleamotu'a

MAEAKAFA'S PROMOTIONS

Maeakafa was performing very well at work. He won a scholarship to study in Fiji. On his return, he was promoted to Corporal Maeakafa Aleamotu'a. He was then required to move with his family into the new Police Training School that had just opened.

The construction of their cement house started at this stage. Later, after another scholarship to study in London, Maeakafa returned to the new position of Inspector of Police and the Head of the Criminal Investigation Department. By then, Lute and Maeakafa's two storey house was ready for them.

Fig 73. Lute and Maekafa's finished home.

CHAPTER 10

*Someone is sitting in the shade today because
someone planted a tree a long time ago.*
Warren Buffet

THE CLOSING OF AN ERA AND
THE DAWN OF THE NEW

When Pesi was visiting her family in Fasi, Mosiana mentioned that the type of Tongan boys their parents approved off included the name Taumoepeau. Pesi was living at Remuera in Auckland at the time, in a student Methodist boarding house for girls. She was always regarded by most of her school classmates as a little sister. At THS she was 3 or 4 years younger than most of her classmates. She was at Auckland University when she met Silivenusi Taumoepeau, the brother of her very close friend at 'Atalanga, Lita Taumoepeau. Venusi went to school at Tonga College and then Wesley College in Auckland before Auckland University. After about a month or so of seeing Venusi he proposed that they get married. Pesi felt sure that her parents would approve of her choice. She got on well with Venusi's sister Lita, so if Venusi was half like her, everything would be fine. Venusi didn't consult his parents either. Pesi had not much idea what Venusi was studying, nor his preferences and lifestyle. All Pesi knew was that his sister and she were quite alike in many respects and that they came from a 'good' and respected family. On reflection now, Pesi thinks Venusi had no idea of her background either. These were definitely not grounds for a 'living happily for ever after' story.

Fig 74. International Students Ball, Auckland University, 1965. front row 3rd from left: Pesi with university staff members.

Pesi explains They planned their wedding. They found a flat in Grafton near the University. Pesi saw Rev R. Clement of the Pitt Street Methodist Church, Auckland, to marry them. Rev R. Clement counselled her against her hasty decision. He asked her if she had spoken with her Dad about it. He said that as a father, he was hesitant to marry them as he considered that they had not thought things through and that Pesi should talk to her Dad first. He knew her Dad was a Methodist Minister. In spite of this, Rev Clement married Pesi and Venusi on 16th September 1967. Paula and Kalolaine Taumoepeau (Dr Samiu Taumoepeau's son and daughter) were their witnesses. Like Lute, no one in Pesi's family knew about her wedding. Venusi's sister Lita, Paula and Kalolaine went with them to a restaurant afterwards to celebrate their wedding.

Pesi graduated with her Mathematics/Science degree at the end of that year and attended Auckland Secondary Teachers Training College for one year. At the beginning of the school year 1969, she started teaching at her old school, Tonga High School. Venusi remained in Auckland to try and complete his studies. Siukimoana

Taumoepeau, their first daughter, was born on 5th April 1969. She was named by her great grandfather Saimone Taumoepeau.

Fig 75i. Siukimoana in Auckland Jan 1970.

Fig 75ii. Mele Helu Sisifa with baby Siukimoana

Fig 76. AUCKLAND GRAMMAR SCHOOL 1966
back row Tongan students l-r: Sefita Hao'uli, Tevita Kolo
second row: 'Alekisanita Sisifa, Paula Taumoepeau
front row: Tu'iono Liava'a, Viliami P. Afeaki. Absent 'Eukalafi Moala.

'ALEKISANITA IN QUEENSLAND

'Aleki attended Auckland Grammar for a year (1966) and stayed at Va'epopua, the residence for the Tongan Scholarship boys near 'Atalanga. After passing his University Entrance Certificate that year, 'Aleki was awarded a Commonwealth Scholarship to study at Queensland Agricultural College. While there, he spent many vacations at Frankston, Victoria, with Mosiana and Bryan where he also worked in farms at Mornington Peninsula, towards his degree.

'Aleki often phoned Pesi to ask how Dad was after she returned to Tonga. 'Aleki asked if he should return home to help with Dad. Pesi explained that Dad had become bedridden. Maybe it made more sense if he completed his course first. They decided that the two of them would pay to get Dad admitted to the Private Hospital adjoining Vaiola Hospital. That way, Dad could be best looked after. In the Tongan custom, daughters do not attend to their own father. Mele

Lahi (Hanipale's daughter) again came to our rescue. She became Dad's personal 'nurse aid'. Dad remained in this Private hospital until a few months before he passed away.

Mele Lahi (Senior) passed away on September 2017 at Utah, USA. Mosiana and Mele attended her funeral. They found that Mele Lahi's Birth Certificate was registered as Mele Helu Sisifa. None of the siblings knew anything about this, whether she just added Sisifa herself by Deed Poll or Mum and Dad registered her at the Birth Registry when she joined the family. This endears her even further to the Sisifa siblings. She was gifted with a happy and jovial disposition and was a most helpful and unforgettable 'sister' to all of us.

On Pesi's return to Tonga, she found the transition from life in

Fig 77. Last photo of Dad that Mosiana took in 1967 during her visit with Bryan and baby Steven.

Auckland to life in Tonga daunting, living with her in-laws in unfamiliar surrounds. Added to that, she started to work as a Senior Maths and Science teacher at THS before taking a short maternity leave. She returned to her job after a few weeks. Next, came juggling work and raising her new born baby. She was absorbed in her little world, inexperienced in Tongan lifestyle as an adult. Fortunately, Venusi's parents Malu, and Seini Taumoepeau and his sisters Saane and 'Ana were very loving grandparents and aunts to Siukimoana.

LUTE AND MAEAKAFA'S MOVE TO THE POLICE TRAINING ACADEMY

Lute's daily responsibilities were more manageable than before when they moved to the Police Training Academy. Lute hired a girl from Havelu, Melania, to be their house-maid. With Dad at the Private Hospital, and Mele Lahi his nurse-aid, Latu went with Lute and Maeakafa to the Police Academy. Mosiana and Bryan took sister Mele to live with them in Frankston, Victoria.

Lute's family's living standard was much improved. Latu had his own room. This enabled him to study more effectively at home. His school results improved tremendously.

FAREWELLING OUR DAD

Our loving Dad passed away peacefully at Lute and Maeakafa's home in Kolomotu'a in early September 1969. He was 55 years old. Present were Lute (25 years old), Pesi (23), Latu (15) and Dad's cousins from Pea.

Dr Tilitili Puloka and Head Matron Sita Heimuli Fineanganofo (daughter of Dad's cousin, Sālote Heimuli) attended to Dad when he passed away.

Fortunately, Lute and Maeakafa had completed building the first stage of their house by the time Dad was brought home from hospital. Their house then was a 3 bedroom, one level cement house. Dad's aunties from Pea, Taumoepenu's sisters, Nunia and Mele Seini came and helped care for Dad before he passed away.

Matapule Taumoepenu received the visitors at Fielakepa's veranda next door to Maeakafa's house.

Rev Tonga Simiki oversaw the running of the kitchen. 'Aleki had wired money for a *pulu* (butchered cow) and other expenses. Rev Harris, President of the Methodist Church, provided money for a *puaka toho* (extra large pig). Malu Taumoepeau, Venusi's dad, sent a *puaka toho* as well. Others arrived with cakes, loaves of bread and provisions for the constant tea making.

Mele Seini, dad's cousin, brought her daughter, Heu, from Pea to be the *fahu* (representative of the presiding aunt of the deceased); and Sela Simiki, Rev Tonga Simiki's wife, took care of the mats, tapa cloths and pieces of material that were brought by the visitors and relatives to pay their respects to Dad. Mele Pua, a cousin of Dad's from Lofanga, then living at Nukunuku, brought their Nukunuku Church Choir to sing throughout the night of Dad's 'apoo (wake). Another Choir from Sia'atoutai (where Dad trained for his ministry and 'Akosī was attending at the time of Dad's funeral) also came to help with the hymn singing.

It was most interesting that Pesi found an undated letter in 2004, written to her by Dad. He wrote the following:

1. His detailed family tree as he remembered it. This is included in Dad's family trees in FT 1 and FT 5.
2. Where he preferred to be buried. The choices for his 'place of rest' were:
   i. Noble Fakafanua's Cemetery at Ma'ufanga opposite the Fāua Wharf by the beach because his dad's grandfather was Kisi Fakafanua.
   ii. Telekava Cemetery in Kolomotu'a, at the section for Church Ministers.

Dad wrote that he preferred his resting place to be at Kolomotu'a since his daughters Lute and Pesi, were married and living in Kolomotu'a. Pesi had no recollection of this letter at the time of his passing. The decision of his burial place was made by the elders and it coincided with his preferred resting place. Also incidentally, the Methodist burial section at Telekava Cemetery, is almost next door to his mother Uaafe's origin, 'Ahoosi. Interestingly, it is opposite to Palu and Nau's home, that we had used on and off as our 'home away from home'.

Fig 78. Muni (Viliami Sisifa) and daughter Lilieta at the graveyard of Rev Sione Finau Sisifa 2017.

Dad's funeral was conducted by Dr 'Amanaki Havea, the Secretary of the Methodist Church at the time, and Dad's classmate at Nafualu College. He became the President of the Methodist Church later. We are most grateful to Rev Harris for his kindness and friendship to Dad right up to his passing.

Fig 79. Rev C. Gribble (Principal TC), Rev G. Harris (President of Wesleyan Church). 1967.

Blessed Assurance, Jesus is mine:	'Oi! keu tala hoku monū!
O what a foretaste of glory divine!	Kuo te ma'u 'a e fanau'i fo'ou.
Heir of salvation, purchase of God;	Hoko 'a e maama ki he po'uli,
Born of His Spirit, washed in His blood.	Hiki 'a e mate ki he mo'ui.
This is my story, this is my song,	Hoku monuué, 'eku koloa,
Praising my Saviour all the day long.	'Ete ongo'i he taimi kotoa
This is my story, this is my song,	Fakamo'oni fakapapau
Praising my Saviour all the day long.	Fale 'a e 'Eiki 'iate au.

FWHB, Tongan Hymn 610, Verse 1. Page 136 Book By Siupeli T. Taliai.

"Kind words and good deeds are eternal. What you have done for yourself alone dies with you; what you have done for others and the community remain forever and are immortal."
By Brian Kahlefeldt.

SIONE FINAU AND MAFI HELU SISIFA'S SIX CHILDREN AND THEIR FAMILIES, AS AT JANUARY 2018

Gradually, as Sione and Mafi's children matured, they became more aware of the special upbringing that their parents strove to give them. They instilled in their children the importance of self-confidence, of love and peaceful co-existence with others, of spiritual awareness and beliefs, of helping those in need. They taught their children that happiness is within themselves and it is in everyday simple activities and thoughts. These mostly unspoken lessons formed a rock-hard footing for their children's lives. Like all caring parents, their children knew that they had been blessed and wished fulfilling and meaningful lives wherever they would be. Sione and Mafi saw at the time, that education was the best means for their children to achieve this end. It is with gratitude and appreciation that their children look back at their journeys since their parents' passed away.

All their six children and grandchildren (bar two), are now living in Australia or New Zealand, enjoying the sort of lives their parents envisaged for them. Through work, the six siblings and their families, have contributed and are contributing to Tonga, Australia and New Zealand. Australia and New Zealand are presently considered the best places on earth in which to live. Melbourne has been ranked 'The Most Livable City in the World' for the past seven consecutive years. This is ahead of Vienna, Vancouver, and Toronto. It is beautiful and peaceful, with an excellent climate. The siblings are not too far from their homeland, Tonga. They can practice their own religion and they are surrounded by many close relatives as well.

Fig 80. Middle Park, after Sione Na'a's and Diana's wedding, 2009. Back row l-r: Mele, Latu, Pesi Front Row: Mosiana, 'Aleki, Lute.

Fig 81. Mosiana's family at Wilsons Promontory Oct 2017. l-r: Lee (carrying 'Ilaisaane), Mele. Back Row: Steven, 'Isileli, Bryan, Jaki, Sione. second row: Olive, Beatrix, Jordi, Moana, Mosiana, Tama, Ziggy. front row: Alia, Michael, Torsten.

Fig 82. 'Ilaisaane, Mosiana's youngest granddaughter, (d Michael Francis) dressed up to dance for grandfather Bryan Francis, on his special birthday in August 2018.

A SUMMARY OF THE LIVES OF THE SIX SISIFA CHILDREN AND THEIR FAMILIES IN EARLY 2018

1. 'Ilaisaane Mosiana Sisifa married Bryan Francis of Rosebud, Australia in May 1966. They have 3 children and 8 grandchildren. All live in Victoria, Australia.

Careers

'Ilaisaane Mosiana Francis: Maamaloa QSC. Retired. Business Owner Clothing Comp.; Receptionist for Minister of Lands; Teacher QSC.

Dr Bryan Francis, Mosiana's husband: Ph.D. Econ. Hist. Retired. Economic Hiastorian; Speech Writer; Head of Accounting Dept., Tafe Teacher.

Dr Tupai Francis, Mosiana's eldest son: Ph.D Migration and Transnationalism. Director at Front Stream; Coord. with Emergency Dept, Vic Red Cross; Lecturer at Melb Uni. Steven's wife.

Beatrix Lombardo Francis, Steven's wife: B.A.; Director at Culture Mate; Bergent Researcher.

Sione Napi Francis, second son of Mosiana: Grad Cert in Museum Studies; BFA, Vic Uni. Artist/Sculptor; Builder. Jaki Gemmell, Sione's partner: Works at Roy Morgan Research.

Michael Francis, youngest son of Mosiana: Electrician and Ranger: Leading Ranger at Port Campbell National Park,Vic. ; Member of the Reserve Defence Force, Aust.

FT6. Mosiana (Sisifa) Francis: Descendents.

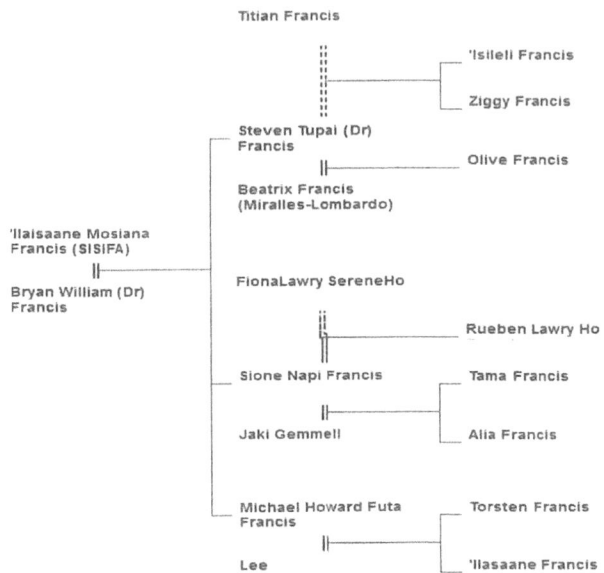

Lou Lee, Michael's partner: Barista and raising 2 children.

All Mosiana's 8 grandchildren are either at school or too young to go to school.

2. Elenoa Lute Sisifa married Maeakafa Aleamotu'a (dc) of Kolomotu'a They have 6 children, 11 grandchildren. Lute migrated to Melbourne in February 2011. Her children migrated in stages to Sydney, Melbourne and New Zealand till early 2011. Her eldest son, Argosy Britania, remains in their home in Tonga and visits Australia regularly. 'Aleki, Latu and Pesi sponsored Lute's move. Mosiana and Bryan helped with finalising Lute's papers .

FT7. Lute (Sisifa) Aleamotu'a: Descendents.

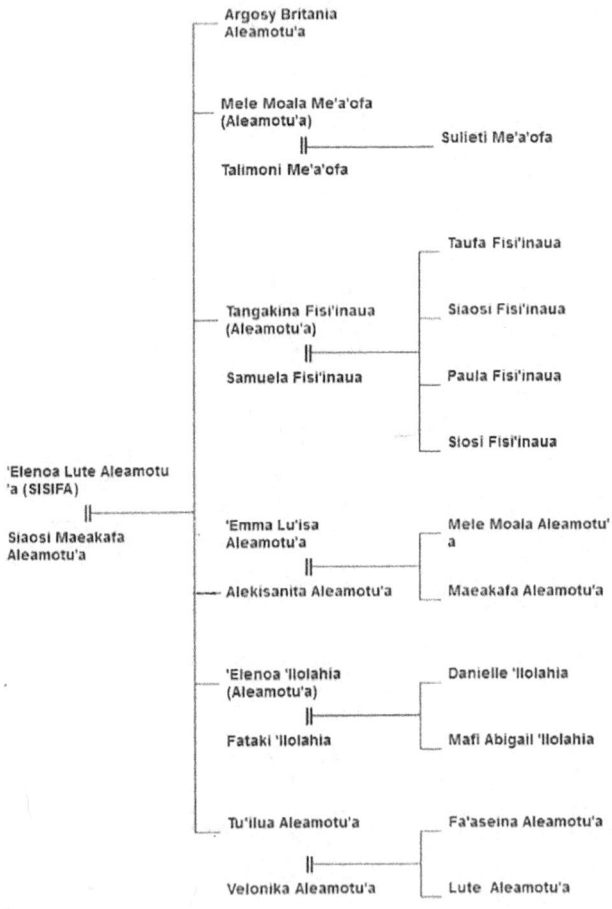

Fig 83. Lute and Maeakafa. 1968.

Fig 84. Mele Moala, Talimoni, Sulieti Me'a'ofa. April, 2014.

Careers

'Elenoa Lute Sisifa Aleamotu'a: Maamaloa, Loumaile, QSC. Retired. Worked for the Tongan Govt July 1964 - 1993. Relieving Senior Exec Officer, Prime Minister's Office; Exec Officer@ Marine

Dept, Min Health, P.O., Inland Revenue, Minister of Police, Minister of Lands, Minister of Finance etc.

Siaosi Maekafa Aleamotu'a, Lute's husband: Chief Superintendent of Police, Tonga.

Mele Moala Aleamotu's Me'a'ofa, Lute's eldest daughter: Tongan Coordinator of Early Childhood Edu, Levin, NZ; Jornalist in Nuku'alofa.

Talimoni Me'a'ofa, Mele Moala's husband: Farm supervisor in Levin, NZ.

Argosy Aleamotu'a, Lute's elder's son: Security with Water Board, Nuku'alofa.

Tangakina Aleamotu'a Fisi'inaua, Lute's second daughter: Volunteer worker, Mercy Hospice, Communicare; Chairperson QSC Ex-Students, NZ; Customer Care, Vodafone; ANZ Bank officer, Tonga.

Fig 85. Tangakina, Samuela, Siosi, back row: Siaosi, Paula, Taufa. 2006.

Fig 86. l-r: Velonika, Tu'ilua, Fa'aseina. 2017.

Fig 87. 'Alekisanita Aleamotu'a. August 2018

Samuela Fisi'inaua, Tangakina's husband: Dip Financial Management. Gen Manager, No.1 Currency/NZ Western Union; ANZ Bank Chief Operation Officer, Honiara, Solomon Is.; ANZ Bank Manager, Tonga.

'Alekisanita Aleamotu'a, Lute's second son: Security in Sydney, Aus.; Accounting Officer, Prime Minister's Office, Tonga.

'Emma Lu'isa Aleamotu'a, 'Alekisanita's wife: Dept of Justice & Attorney Gen. Sydney, Aust.

Zuel Tu'ilua 'i Faletuikapai Aleamotu'a, Lute's youngest son: Gas Station operator, Auckland; Clerk at Ministry of Finance, Nuku'alofa.

Velonika Aleamotu'a, Tu'ilua's wife: studying to be a teacher.

'Elenoa Aleamotu'a 'Ilolahia, Lute's youngest daughter: B. Nursing: Nurse, Northern Hospital, Melbourne; Nurse, Vaiola Hospital, Tonga.

Fataki 'Ilolahia, 'Elenoa's husband: Head Chef , Mr Wolf Restaurant, Melb.; Accountant, Ministry of Finance, Tonga.

Fig 88. 'Elenoa, Mafi, Fataki, Danielle 'Ilolahia. 15-7-2018.

Fig 89. Lute jr, Fa'aseina Aleamotu'a.2018.

Fig 90. Argosy Brittania, 2015.

Fig 91. 'Aleki Aleamotua's family: Maeakafa, Yvette, Mele Moala, Lu'isa.

'ILISAPESI LINA WEIR

Lute has 11 grandchildren: 7 are still at school or too young to attend school.

Taufa Fisi'inaua, Tangakina's eldest son: Actor.

Siaosi Fisi'inaua, Tangakina's second son: studying to be a musician; working in Building Industry.

Paula Fisi'inaua, Tangakina's third son: studying Law; working in Building Industry.

Siosi Fisi'inaua, Tangakina's daughter and youngest child: Year 12: Hoping to study Medicine.

3. 'Ilisapesi Lina Sisifa, married Silivenusi Taumoepeau of Kolofo'ou. They had 2 daughters before they divorced and Pesi moved with their girls to Melbourne in April 1972. Pesi then married David John Gordon Weir on 23 January 1979 thereby added 3 step-sons to her family. David (dc 17 April 2017) had 6 grandchildren and 1 great granddaughter from his three sons.

Fig 92. Moana's admission to the Bar, April 1992. Pesi, Moana, David.

Fig 93. Moana and Marcel, Nov 1996

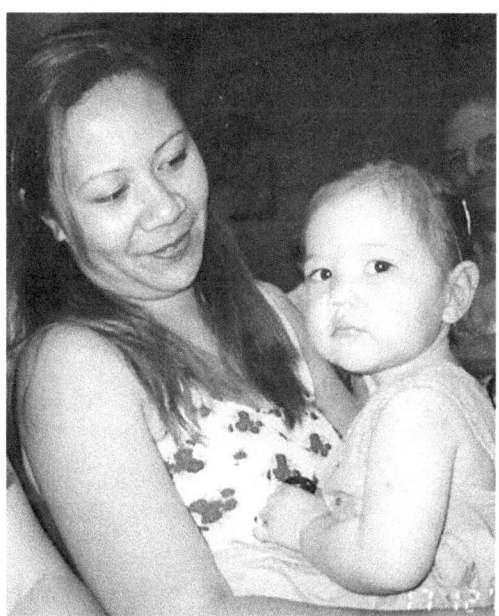

Fig 94. Mafi and Dana, Dec 2001.

Careers

'Ilisapesi Sisifa Weir: B.Sc, Cert IV Finance and Mortgage Broking. Retired. Owner Property Real Est. Business. President of Professional Women's Zonta Club, ACT; Parish Council Weston Anglican Church and St Luke's Anglican Church, Sth Melbourne, VIC; Maths and Science Teacher at Tonga High School; 45 years teaching with leadership roles in Public and Private Sec Schools in VIC and ACT.

David J.G. Weir, 'Ilisapesi's husband: Awarded Paul Harris Fellow By Rotary Dist 9820, Mt Eliza. Management Overseas Charitable Organisations: Care Aus, Cambodia; Laos; Yemeni; Darogetti Children in Nairobi; Feed the Children in Kenya; Country and Action Aid in Bangladesh; Sales Manager, Golden Fleece.

Moana Weir (Siukimoana Taumoepeau), 'Ilisapesi's eldest daughter: B.Law Honours. Managing Director, Bupa Dental Corporation; Chair of Human Rights and Egual Opportunities, Vic; Bupa Legal Director, NZ and Regulatory; Gen Counsel and Company Secretary for ASX-listed Companies including REA (realestate.com.au) and SEEK; Lawyer in top tier legal Firms and in house at Coles Myer.

Dr Marcel Van Der Schoot, Moana's ex husband: Ph.D Chemistry: Project Leader@Centre for Aust Weather and Climate and with CSIRO. Reseacher & International Lecturer @ CSIRO, Bureau of Meterology, Aust Div Marine & Atmospheric Research.

Fig 95. Mafi and Craig at Moana's wedding, Nov 1996.

Fig 96. Lina, Dana, Jordi, March 2017. Dana's PCW Graduation.

Mafi Angelina Weir (Mafi Taumoepeau), 'Ilisapesi's Youngest daughter: Worked in Sales with Myers and Babyco.

Craig Allen, Mafi's partner: Retired injured Gunner, Australian Army.

FT8. 'Ilisapesi (Sisifa) Weir: Descendents.

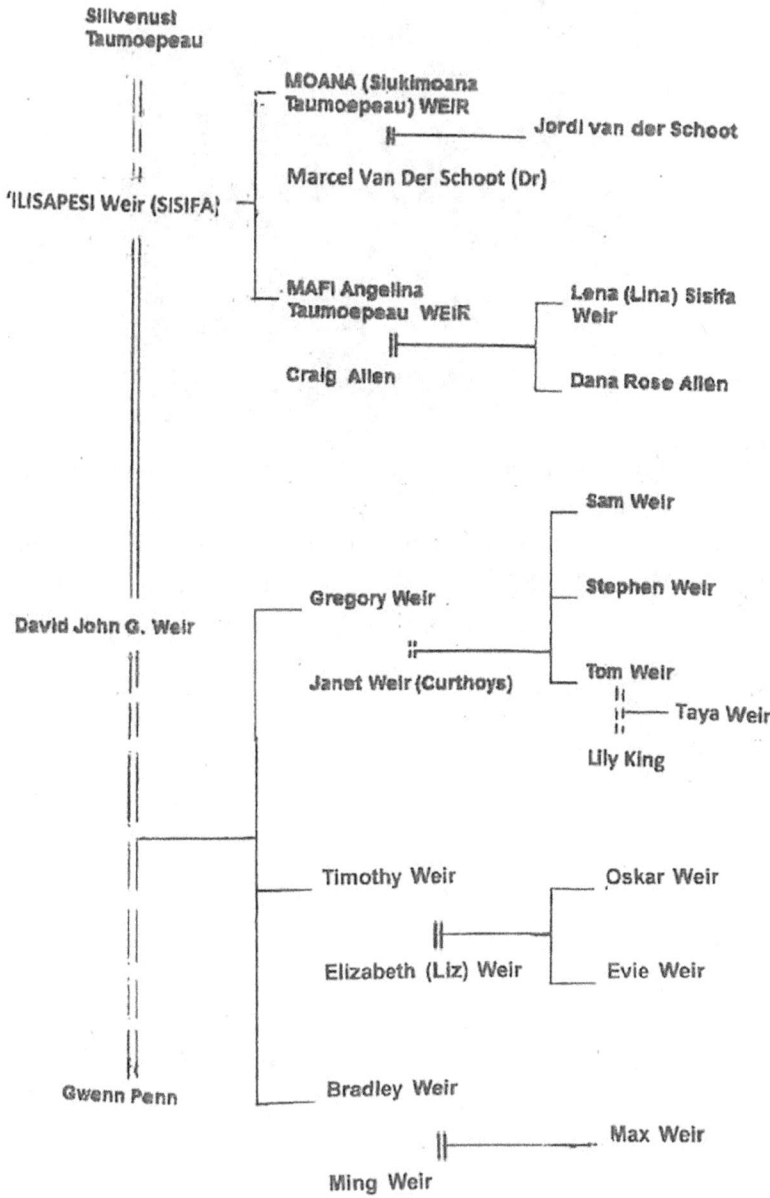

Pesi has 3 grandchildren

Lina Sisifa Weir, Mafi's eldest daughter: Project Manager at Pivot Const. Group and studying Construction Management and Finance.

Dana Rose Allen, Mafi's second daughter: Studying Health (undecided as to her field) and working as a Gym Instructor.

Jordi Van Der Schoot, Moana's son: 10 years old.

Fig 97. Siulolo and 'Alekisanita at Setaleki and Belinda's wedding 2012.

Fig 98. Palu and Fiona Sisifa with Moana Weir (middle) at one of Palu's celebratory dinners, 2016.

Fig 99. 'Aleki and his boys, Jan 4th 2013. l-r:
'Aleki jr, Sione F, 'Ilaisa Futa, 'Aleki Sr, Matini.

4. 'Alekisanita Uinoa-i-Hakau Sisifa (dc) married Siulolo Fangafua Nau of Kolofo'ou. They moved to Auckland, New Zealand before 2000. They have 6 children and 4 grandchildren. Siulolo's mother sponsored 'Aleki's family's move.

'Alekisanita Sisifa (dc 12 April 2004): B. Appl.Sci. (Rural Tech); Cert in Agriculture; Cert in Management; International Training Inst, Aust. 'Aleki worked for SPC and United Nations from 2000-2014 (right up to his passing). Previously, he worked for Secretariat of the Pacific Community (SPC) in Agriculture and Forestry; then Food and Agric. Organaisation of the UN on secondment from Tonga in 2000 until he retired. He worked at Agric, Fisheries and Forrests in Tonga 1974-1997. Siulolo Fangafua Sisifa, 'Aleki's wife: Hotel Management, Auckland.

Fig 100. Sione and Sālote Sisifa's family. l-r: Viliami, Sione, Sālote, 'Ilisapesi, Jared, Fua. 2018.

Sione Finau Sisifa, 'Alekisanita's eldest son: LL.M. Auckland, Solicitor General, President of Tonga Legal Soc.; Previously Attorney General, Tonga.

Salote Sisifa, Sione's wife: Journalist and Sports Manager (Netball)/Publicist, Tonga.

Matini Sisifa, 'Alekisanita's second son: IT specialist, Auckland.

Dinalee Uhi Sisifa: Hotel Industry.

Fiona Sisifa, 'Alekisanita's eldest daughter: M.Sc. : Marketing.

Fig 101. Mātini and Dinah Sisifa with Princess Pilolevu. 2016.

Dr Palu Sisifa, 'Alekisanita's second daughter: Ph.D International Business Management: Lecturer/Reseacher at Auckland University.

'Alekisanita Jr Sisifa, 'Alekisanita's third son. Enjoys life and works occassionally!

'Ilaisa Futa Sisifa: B.Agriculture.

'Alekisanita has 4 grandchildren.

3 are at Tonga High School: Viliami, 'Ilisapesi and Jared.

Fangafua is 2 years old.

FT9. 'Alekisanita Uinoaihakau Sisifa: Descendents.

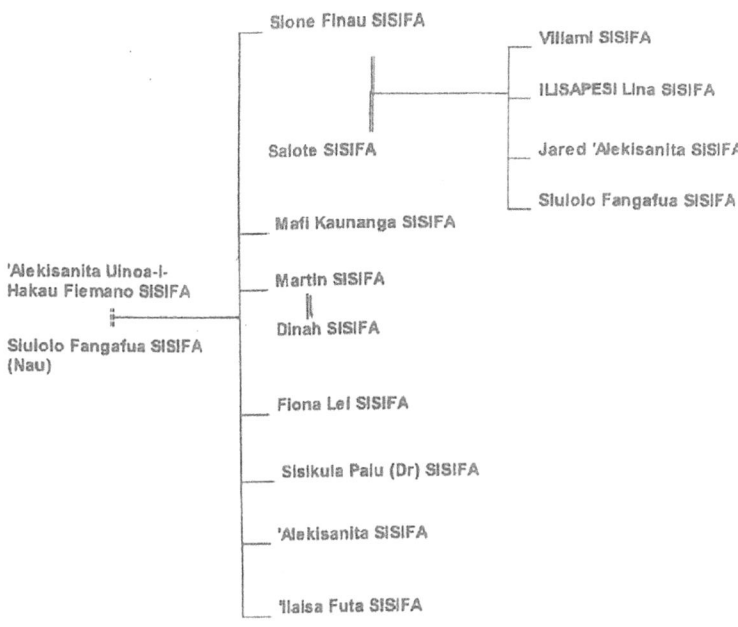

Fig 102. Mele Teufolau Sisifa 2017.

5. Mele Teufolau Sisifa immigrated to Melbourne, Australia in 1967 sponsored by Mosiana and Bryan. She is mother and grandmother to all Mosiana and Bryan's brood. She is aunt and grandaunt to Mosiana's children and grandchildren and to all our children and grandchildren.

Mele Teufolau Sisifa: Potter. Retired Supervisor at Ingham's Enterprises.

Fig 103. l-r: Dr Latu, Kilisitina, Pesi, Belinda, Setaleki at Dr Steven Sisifa's graduation, ACT 2016.

6. Sione Latu Vaihumoa Sisifa married Kilisitina Fiefia. They migrated to Melbourne, Australia in 1991.

They have 4 children and 5 grandchildren. Pesi sponsored his family's move to Melbourne.

Dr Sione Sisifa: Medical Doctor. Medical Practitioner in Melbourne Clinics.

Kilisitina Fiefia Sisifa, Sione Latu's wife: Translator Tongan-Eng: Member of Uniting Church Parish Councils.

Nuia Sisifa Senituli, Latu's adopted daughter,: B.A. Health industry.

Richmond Senituli, Nuia's husband.

Setaleki Sisifa, Latu's eldest son: Physiotherapist in Melbourne.

Belinda Sisifa, Setaleki's wife: Fulltime mum.

Sione Na'a Sisifa, Latu's second son: Accountant and Business Manager.

Fig 104. Elizabeth, Nuia and Richmond, 2011.

Fig 105. Sione Na'a and Diana, 2011.

Fig 106. Dr Steven Sisifa at his graduation, 2016.

Diana Sisifa, Sione Na'a's wife: Legal Administrator.

Dr Steven Sisifa, Latu's third son: Medical Practitioner in Canberra, ACT.

Latu and Kilisitina have 4.98 grandchildren. Only Elizabeth goes to school.

FT10. Sione Latu Sisifa: Descendents

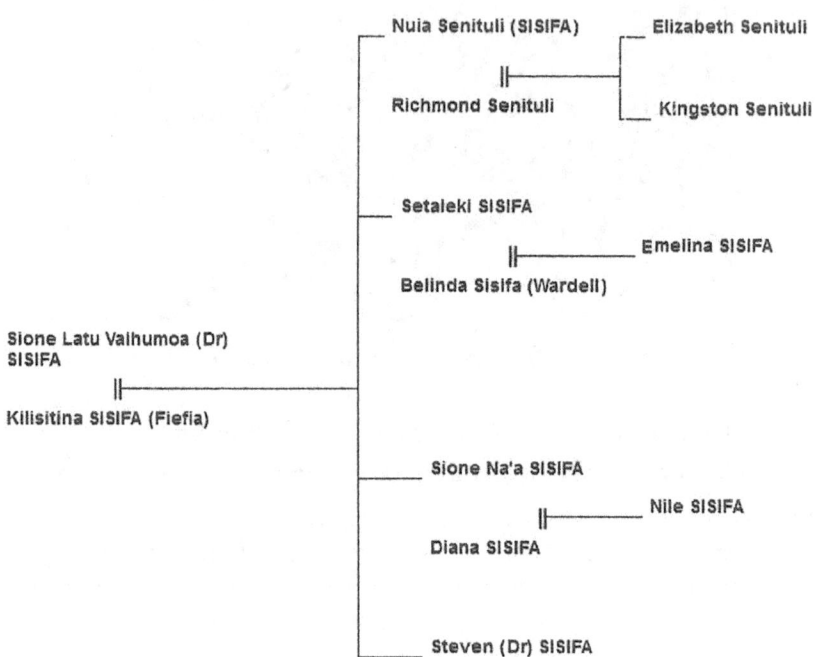

Fig 107. LATU AND KILISITINA'S FAMILY, CHRISTMAS 2017.
Standing at left of stairs, from the back: Latu, Belinda, Kilisitina.
Sitting, from the back, l-r: Setaleki, Sione Na'a, Steven,
Richmond, Elizabeth, 'Emelina. Front row: Nile, Diana.

IN TRIBUTE TO 'ALEKISANITA UINOA-'I-HAKAU FIEMANO SISIFA. DIED APRIL 2014 IN AUCKLAND

'Aleki's writing on parts of his work in Tonga. April 2004.

My first visit (to Kolovai) was in the early 1980s for the official opening of agricultural offices and residences for the Ministry of Agriculture and Forestry in the island. Mr Tomasi Simiki who was the Director of Agriculture at the time, was away on leave and I was the most senior officer in Tonga. Thus I had to do the honours. The second time was when the then 'Olovaha' ferry was commissioned by HM Taufa'ahau Tupou IV. We visited Niuafo'ou and Niuatoputapu, spending two days each on these islands.

On three separate occasions I was to accompany HM King Taufa'ahau Tupou IV on his Agricultural (and later also Industrial) Shows covering the whole country. The first time was in 1983 and was of particular significance to me. The country was flattened by Cyclone Isaac in the previous year. The King decided that because one year was not enough for the population to rehabilitate their farms and get good produce at the same time, an inspection of the countryside was a more appropriate way of showing his concern. In Ha'apai, the show party on Government vehicles toured the whole of Foa from Lotofoa to Fangale'ounga/Fotua as well as Lifuka. We then went on the *MV Late* to Kauvai, the minimoke taking the King and Queen and all others, me included, walking the main road from the middle of the island where the wharf landing was to the other end of the island. Presentations to HM were shouted from beside the road and appropriately responded to – albeit in summarised form – by Matapules on the move, asking them to take the pigs, kava and food to the wharf landing for loading on to the *MV Late*.

The next day we visited 'Uiha island, an occasion also for the King to officially open a wharf. A big feast was held at the *Mala'e* (town park or meeting place), complete with a number of the traditional dances, *lakalaka* etc. Overall, food gardens in Ha'apai were well on their way to being rehabilitated. The effort of the M.A.F. in this regard, particularly in ploughing the land and quickly multiplying planting material, was obviously successful.

Fig 108. 'Aleki, Tongan Acting Director of Agriculture accompanying King Taufa'ahau IV, followed by Ministers of the Crown, at the Agricultural Show, Teufaiva Showground.

Fig 109. 'Aleki with Lord Vaea visiting Rome on business.

Then the show party left for Niuafo'ou via Vava'u on the '*Olovaha*'. The farms in Niuafo'ou looked great and vanilla as a new cash generating venture stood out as a potentially strong part of the Niuafo'ou farming system.

An event occurred in Niuatoputapu that was to be a topic of jest in later years. The Royal party had arrived in Niua on a Friday. The King had agreed to take the island tour on Saturday morning. The tour party was small. On the big German made high Unimoke were King Taufa'ahau Tupou IV, Queen Halaevalu Mata'aho, Aide de Camp, Baron Vaea's son and the driver. On the mini moke was myself and my driver, the 76 six year old Tu'iniua Finau. Somewhere in the interior of Niua, the engine of the Unimoke spluttered and died. The driver toiled under the heavy vehicle for over an hour and it was close to midday with temperature climbing to uncomfortable levels. By about 1.00pm, the Aide de Camp told me the King wants to drink a coconut. I looked around there were only two palms nearby, one was small and had no fruits and the other must have been over thirty feet tall with about 4 fruits tucked away on the top part of the fronds. In due course, I could hear a small sound much like the motorcycle that it was. It was Agriculture Officer, Mr Piutau Tupou, aged 48, 15 years my senior with a paunch that stood out on its own like a hill in Tongatapu. To cut a long story short, Piutau climbed and worked hard to get the one coconut down then a little way down, got the message that the Queen would like a coconut as well. Piutau got that down then practically slid down, having lost all control of his arms and legs. He lost a certain amount of flesh from his stomach, chest, arm and leg areas. Over bowls of kava in Niuatoputapu, Mr Tupou got installed with the Matapule name of *'Mamulu ma'ae Hau'* ('Grazed in the Service of the Supreme Chief'). To this day I am not sure whether he was proud of that name or not.'

In memory of Aleki Sisifa (1948–2014)

"Small is the voice of the chief, for gentleness and courtesy should walk hand in hand with power"

Aleki Sisifa devoted his working life to strengthening food security in the Pacific region and to improving the lot of the smallholder farmers who underpin it. He was a natural leader, with an uncanny ability to unite disparate team members from all disciplines and walks of life, finding consensus and delivering optimum development outcomes for the region. A true Pacific Chief and mentor to so many, he will not be forgotten.

Fig 110. A Tribute to 'Alekisanita Sisifa. author: Co-worker at SPC (South Pacific Community), Fiji.

Fig 111. AT 'ALEKISANITA'S BURIAL, April, 2014 Sisifa Cousins Viliami, Suli, Sione; Mele, Bryan Francis, Latu, Sione Sisifa ('Aleki's eldest son).

Fig 112. UNVEILING 'ALEKISANITA'S HEADSTONE, April 2015. l-r: Lose Helu Jenner, Dr Latu, Saimone Helu, Penisimani Finau, Pesi, Mele, Mosiana, Uaafe, Tangakina, Siulolo.

Fig 113. DR PALU SISIFA VISITS HER DAD'S MALA'E AFTER HER GRADUATION CEREMONY IN APRIL 2016. l-r: Her aunties and mum. Peta, Pesi, Palu, Siulolo, Mosiana, Seilose.

Fig 114. 'ALEKI AND SIULOLO'S CELEBRATORY DINNER FOR PALU'S GRADUATION. Princess Pilolevu and Lord Tuita were guests of honour. April 2016.

IN MEMORY OF MUNI (VILIAMI SISIFA), 1947 – NOVEMBER 2018

By Lute Aleamotu'a

Before Dad retired from his ministry at Fasi, Viliami 'drifted off' for a period of time. He kept company with two other young boys of his age. One night they broke into the Water Board shop and took construction materials. They were caught and they had to appear in Court. On the night before the court case, Viliami had a dream that he met Dad coming towards him outside the Magistrate Court. Dad explained to Viliami in his dream, that he was to plead guilty and admit all that had happened on the night of the crime.

In Court, after following Dad's instructions from his dream, Viliami was directed by the presiding Magistrate to 'catch the next boat to Lofanga, go and till the land, attend church and follow the teachings of Christ.' The other two of the gang were sent to prison to serve out their punishment.

Back in Lofanga, Viliami became a reliable and hardworking disciple of Christ and a humble God loving citizen of Tonga. After his own father passed away, Viliami was given the title Muni by the Tu'i Pelehake of the time. Rev Sione Finau's family is most grateful to Viliami for his selfless giving to them and to all who knew him later in his life. He devoted a lot of his later life to teaching everyone around him how to deliver a '*malanga*' (Christian message from the Bible). He even learnt to use a laptop to type out series of malanga for those in the USA, New Zealand and Australia that needed them. Despite his suffering from severe pain from arthritis, he continued to be a kind, loving and giving individual right to the end, dying in a church while delivering a sermon. He is sorely missed by all who crossed his path.

CHAPTER 11

Tales from the South Pacific Kingdom
of Tonga shaping the Lives of
Rev Sione Finau and Mafi Helu Sisifa.

MIGRATIONS AND ANCIENT TONGAN RELIGION

From archaeological and genetic evidences, about 400,000 years ago, the 'Two Routes For Human Evolution' left Africa. The Alternate Model at the bottom of Fig 115 is believed to have taken place about 60,000 years ago. Source Google and DNA research.

Further to archaeological and genetics evidence, linguistics and behavioural patterns point to the Polynesian race having come via Iran, through South East Asia and the East Indies. It's also found that some may have come via Taiwan. Of particular interest, are striking similarities between Polynesians and the Taiwanese Aborigines. See book published by Kaiser et al in 2008.

Further evidences also led to the belief that Polynesians landed in Samoa first. Some then left from there and found Hawaii. Some found Tahiti. Consequentially, some from Tahiti, travelled south and landed in New Zealand in about 1350 AD (the Maoris). The Tongans and the Cook Islanders started to sail south from Samoa in about year 950 AD. The Tongans and Samoans display the closest resemblance to each other of all Polynesians as they are very close geographically. Inter-marriage between them continues to date.

The Iran connection may explain the strict adherence of Tongans to the 'tabu' custom, similar to the Biblical *Hebrew custom*. The frequent foray by Japanese to the Pacific islands could explain the Tongans' similarity of divisions in society into 'spiritual rulers' or 'human deity' and commoners.

The following account of the history of Tonga was drawn from the book HGT.

European contact with Tonga began on 9th May 1616 with Jan Schouten and Jacob Lemaire (Dutch discoverers who discovered and named Cape Horn on the same trip). In searching for a great southern continent, they accidently came across Niuatoputapu. The next visitor was another Dutch discoverer, Able Tasman, who was sent to explore New Holland (Dutch name for Australia). On 21st January 1643, Able Tasman reached the island 'Eua to the east of Tongatapu. He stopped briefly in Hihifo (Tongatapu) and Nomuka (Ha'apai). He saw neither weapons nor temples and assumed Tongans had no religion and wars were unknown here. (It happened to be a time of peace and prosperity in Tonga.)

Of the many gods whom the Tongans held in awe, the chief ones were: *Tangaloas* in the sky, *Mauis* in the underworld, and *Hikule'o* who presided over *Pulotu* (paradise which was beyond the sunset in the western ocean). All chiefs were immortal and their souls after death went to Pulotu (commoners had no souls). The spirits in Pulotu had great power and when the need arose, sacrifices were taken to the priests' houses for prayers to the spirits in Pulotu.

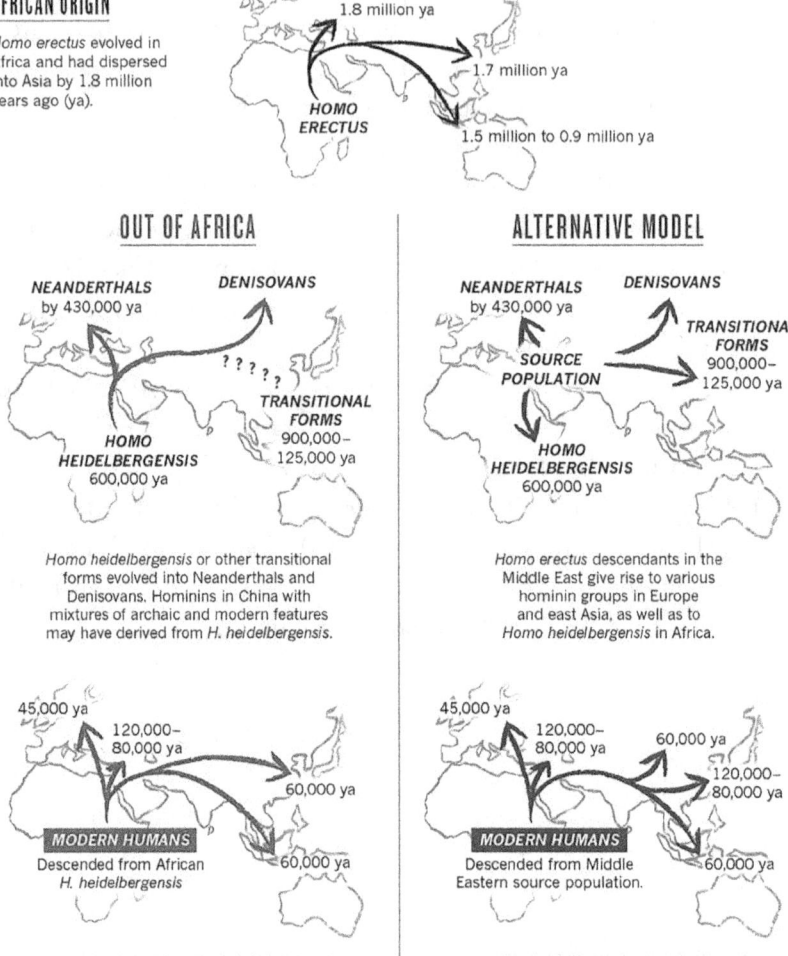

Fig 115. Two Routes For Human Evolution

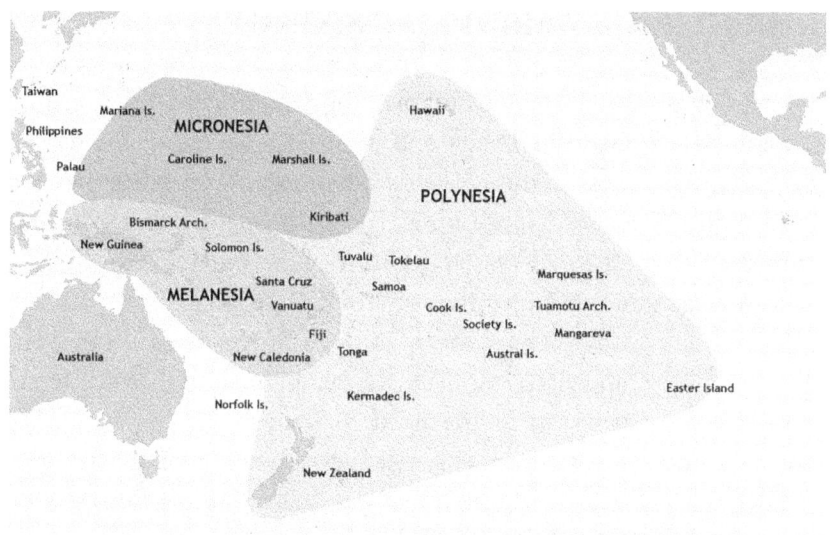

Fig 116. The Polynesian spread of colonizasion throughout the Polynesian Triangle - Kayser 2000, 20008

The Tu'i Tonga (Sacred King) was the High Priest of *Hikule'o* (Paradise), a direct descendent of the gods. Hence the esteem respect that Tongans gave their King and *Hou'eiki* (chiefs). The first Tu'i Tonga was 'Aho'eitu (about year 950 AD). Important names and descendants were preserved via poems and songs throughout the generations.

When Captain Cook first visited Tonga in 1773, he was very impressed by the orderly way in which vegetable plantations and fruit trees were planted and maintained. In Hihifo (West), he observed that most gardens were enclosed by fences made of reeds and that there were wide roads constructed which branched off into smaller ones and led into the plantations. He was also intrigued by the intricacies and hierarchical structure of Tonga's society. He did not fully understand it but recorded in detail and 'without bias', everything that he observed. There were no fortifications or defences between plantations at this time.

CHRISTIANITY ARRIVED IN TONGA

As a result of the favourable impressions and relationships Captain Cook made in Tonga and Tahiti, he encouraged England to send missionaries to these islands. Missionaries started arriving in both countries in 1797. Unfortunately, as it happened, this coincided with the period of 'Civil War and Disorder' in Tonga, 1797-1826.

A huge struggle for supremacy took place between the various High Chiefs who were brothers, sons and/or cousins of the Tu'i Tonga, Tu'i Ha'atakalaua and Tu'i Kanokupolu. The three different royal lineages arose out of the need to remove the higher ranked person from everyday business. The new Religion of Christianity further complicated the division between the various factions.

In addition to the book HGT, the following short historical account was sourced from the book, TCSH, recently published in June 2016. It was fortuitous that this major work was published when it did, as it assisted Lute and Pesi to more fully understand and appreciate the evolving background that developed and shaped their parents' principles and strong faith.

When the Civil Wars (1826 -1845) subsided, Aleamotu'a (Siosaia Tupou) was made Tu'i Kanokupolu

Taufa'ahau, ruler of Ha'apai was the standout young man of the day. He doubted the Tongan gods and started supporting the new faith. Others joined him in time. He was impatient to learn to read books, understand English, and to learn about Christianity very quickly. He secured himself a teacher, a Tongan preacher (Pita Vi) from Nuku'alofa who had learnt basic reading and writing. Pita arrived in Ha'apai from Tongatapu with pens and paper. Rev John Thomas arrived in Ha'apai a few months later in 1830 to teach Taufa'ahau. To his amazement, he found that this Ruler of Ha'apai and some others could already read and write.

On 7 August 1834, Taufa'ahau was baptized as Siaosi (or George after the King of England) and he retained one of his wives, as his Christian wife Sālote (Charlotte, named after the Queen of

England). The ruler of Vava'u, Finau 'Ulukalala died in 1833, after naming Taufa'ahau as his successor.

In Tongatapu, Chief Tu'ivakano became a Christian together with many commoners. King Aleamotu'a apparently had a weak personality. When he heard that chiefs from *Hahake* (East of Tongatapu) were to attack him, he sought help from the Ha'apai Ruler, Taufa'ahau. Taufa'ahau arrived from Ha'apai, fought and negotiated peace successfully. Before King Aleamotu'a's death in 1845, he told Tungi, the great chief of Mu'a that he wished for Taufa'ahau to succeed him. Those with claims for the position of King or Ruler of Tongatapu were Mumui, son of Tupoumalohi; Ma'afu'otu'itonga, son of Aleamotu'a; and Taufa'ahau, son of Tupouto'a Tuku'aho. The electing chiefs were unanimous in their selection of Taufa'ahau to be the rightful Tu'i Kanokupolu on the grounds of descent and personal qualities. In 1845, Taufa'ahau was installed as Tu'i Kanokupolu, King George Tupou 1.

King George Tupou 1 was a visionary for his people. He craved for knowledge. In his sermons (recorded by Rev Robert Young in 'Southern World') he encouraged his subjects to "observe the difference between the white men and the men of this land! Are they born wiser or are they more capable? No, they obtained knowledge from the 'Book'"!

King George Tupou 1 kept asking for a visit to Sydney to observe how things were done in the 'big world'. He got his chance in 1853 when Rev Robert Young offered him passage on the mission ship John Wesley. The Sydney Morning Herald on Christmas Eve 1853, reported him as saying:

'When in my own land, the missionaries used to tell me and my people of what God has done in England and elsewhere, we have listened with very great interest. Some of us believed and some did not: and I therefore resolved in my mind to come and see this land. I found on my arrival that all I had heard previously were but a little thing compared with what I have seen since. I found that everything I had heard was perfectly true, and, like the Queen of the South, I found that only half had been told me.'

King Tupou 1 recognised right from the beginning, the crucial importance of education. The first school was established at Hihifo in 1826 by Missionary Rev John Thomas from England. King Tupou 1 pushed the Wesleyan Church hard to send him a College man to teach his people. He asked specifically for the young Headmaster of Newington College at the time, James Egan Moulton.

Finally, the King's wish was granted and James Egan Moulton and his new wife Emma arrived in Nuku'alofa on 28 May 1865.

The Chairman of the District, Rev John Whewell, had been in Tonga for about 10 years and he had a very negative view of the standard reached then. He complained to J.E. Moulton, "The people had remained ignorant and they failed to produce 'a vernacular literature'". In spite of this, within a very short time, J. E. Moulton increased the number of text books in the Tongan language. Over the years, Moulton worked tirelessly with his tutors to produce an impressive store of literature 'in the grand old Tongan language' and these have proven priceless in educating Tongans to date. TCSH page 33.

Fig 117. The Moulton Family. back row: Henrieta Grace, William, Vuna Alfred front row: James Egan, Emma, Dr Moulton, Mary Knight (Melenaite) and Mary. source tcsh.

In 1855, Tupou 1 signed a Treaty for Peace and Friendship with Napoleon 111, the French Emperor, between Tonga and France. The Code of 1862, The First Parliament and the 'Emancipation of the People' all took place in 4 June 1862. A Treaty with Germany was signed on 1st November 1876. Treaties were signed with Britain (1879) and America (1888). Historians all agree that King George Tupou 1 had given Tonga a strong foundation to see it through to the twentieth century. King George Tupou 1 died in 1893 at the age of 96. He had outlived 3 generations. His great grandson acceded as King George Tupou 11 in 1893. He proved to be extremely intelligent and very well informed.

Fig 118. Rev. Rodger Page and Queen Sālote during one of her visits to Sydney in the early 1960s. source tcsh

On 18 May 1900, King Tupou 11 signed a 'Treaty of Friendship and Protection' between Britain and Tonga.

Because of this, during the First World War, even though German warships were in the Pacific, they left Tonga alone. In 1916, the Treaty of Friendship with Germany was annulled and German firms in Tonga were closed. A few business German families remained in Tonga. Mum and Dad were born during this period.

Princess Sālote became HM Queen Sālote Tupou 111 in 1918 on the death of her father, King George Tupou 11, just as the First World War ended. HM Queen Sālote was the successful ruler of Tonga from 11th October 1918 till 16th December 1965 (48 years). She steered Tonga successfully in local matters as well as in international affairs between the two World Wars and after World War II and its undesirable consequences on her people. She used trusted political advisers such as Rev Rodger Page, to her and her country's advantage.

The 'stage' was set for Mafi Helu and Sione Finau Sisifa to grow up in this 'newly established' Christian environment and College education system.

THE LIVES OF REV SIONE FINAU SISIFA AND MAFI ANGAHIKI HELU SISIFA RECOLLECTIONS BY REV LOPETI TAUFA

Rev Lopeti Taufa, Retired Ex-President of The Weslyan Methodist Church of Tonga, wrote the following in response to a request by Lute and Mele Moala Aleamotu'a. 7th August 2004.

"Sione of Tupou College"

The marriage of Mafi and Sione was a partnership of intellectuals. They were perfectly matched in every way.

Their lives were inspired by their Christian Faith and Education. They devoted their lives to God and the Church.

Lofanga belonged to the *Siasi Fakaongo* (the church that was part of the Australasian Wesleyan Methodist in Australia). The Wesleyan Church of Tonga split into Siasi Fakaongo and a new faction called "Wesleyan Free Church of Tonga" in 1886. The new faction was controlled locally in Tonga under King Tupou 1. The people of Lofanga were persecuted for refusing to change their allegiance. (TCSH P79). Sione grew up surrounded by people of great faith. Sione's roots were planted by forebears who were persecuted, deported or starved to death for their steadfast beliefs. Nearby islands Kotu and Lotofoa, in Ha'apai, also refused to change their allegiance to the new church and pledged to support the original Church. Sione anchored his youth in the Weslyan Church College. He was a prefect and a preacher. He was a trusted and responsible student. He continued there as a teacher, got married and worked as a *Faifekau* until he retired.

Sione was one of the *Faifekaus* at the time, who qualified very young at Nafualu. Rev Page was the President of the Weslyan Church then. Rev Page counselled Sione to find a wife immediately. That evening, a party accompanied him to where Mafi was (*Kolovai 'api faifekau*, with cousin Neomai Helu and Rev 'Ikani Taliai) to ask Mafi to marry him. Mafi was a most suitable match for Sione.

Both Sione and Mafi studied for their Government Teacher Certificates at Nafualu and QSC at the same time as their academic certificates. Later, Tonga College opened at 'Atele, and a separate Government Teacher Training College was also opened. Nafualu and QSC abandoned their Teacher Training courses then. Sione received Maamaloa and Teacher College Certificate in 1936, and Loumaile later (score of 75% or more in the final exams) before teaching at Nafualu and Kolovai Church Primary School. Mafi received her Maamaloa and Teacher Training College Certificate in the same year (1938) and taught at a Primary School for a year before teaching at QSC.

Lopeti emphasised the effect of Mafi's and Sione's good upbringing in everything they did. Mafi grew up in Lotofoa in a highly educated and fairly well to do family (Helu) and attended Queen Sālote College. Sione was brought up in Lofanga where it's people were renowned for their extreme forward planning, frugal living and hard working.

During Sione's and Mafi's term in Hihifo, Lopeti Taufa was teaching at Vaipoa, Niuatoputapu.

While Sione and Mafi were the Faifekau Pule (Head Minister) in Hihifo, they were lauded for the way they led and ministered to the people under their care. All matters spiritual, financial and material were handled with skill and real concern. The Church absolutely thrived under Sione's guidance. The opening of the Centenary Church of Nuku'alofa, saw a large choir from Niua attend the celebrations. Post Master, Malekamu Manu was its conductor. Sione and Mafi were both natural leaders and were well loved by their congregation.

CHILD REARING

The way they tended their church family was the same as how they cared for their own children. The children had set routines for study, small chores, family prayers, play time and so on.

Every weekday evening, the children had a homework session, then they packed away their books and pencils and placed them in their set places ready for the morning. In the morning, the children cleaned their faces and teeth, sat at the kitchen ready for breakfast. Sione or Mafi would say a prayer (not just 'grace') before their breakfast. Bread, baked by Mafi, and tea were set up beforehand, observed Lopeti.

Lopeti also observed how small duties, like collecting the books after study time, were assigned between the children. He noted the *haiane malala* (iron heated with coal from coconut shells) was used to iron their clothes. The kitchen (*peito*) was constructed of tin and the table was adequate for the family. The 'home altar' was the dinner table. This was subsequently adopted by the church in Tonga as the morning 'home altar' and is in memory of Sione and Mafi.

Vaipoa village is in between Hihifo and Falehau. Lopeti said that when he arrived in Vaipoa as a teacher, there were only 6 local students at the Church Primary School. Most of the students were from Hihifo and Falehau. They included: Voka, Pongi, Tanaki and Hau, 'Atelaite and Taufa Savelio. Lopeti remembered Mosiana, Lute, Pesi and 'Aleki (4 years old), attending his school. The school was in a long building and students were divided into 4 classes. Mosiana was in Class 4, and 'Aleki in Class 1. The children's clothes were immaculate as Mafi took a lot of care dressing them. Their food was always carefully prepared and packed into a cloth bag. Every day they were accompanied to school by their little dog. He noticed Lute always took great care with her appearance. Sione's appearance was always immaculate as well. Lopeti contrasted the appearance of these children, to that of Moka's children, Fifita and Telua, who appeared *"nonoa'ia pe 'i honau 'api"* (disorganised and lacking purpose as at home). He noted that Mosiana and Pesi had excellent writing. 'Aleki was too young to manage writing. Lute was not yet proficient (this was of course due to her left-handedness and being forced to use her right hand instead). Mosiana was a very neat student. Mafi and Sione taught her to use a ruler to divide her pages into sections. Once Lute absented herself from choir practice and she was punished (caned) for it. Lopeti noticed how Mafi always took extra care with 'Aleki in everything in which he was involved.

According to the girls, 'Aleki was *'anga faka'ofa'* (mild and conciliatory mannered) from birth. They all adored him as well. They thought that Dad, as much as he loved his girls, he really appreciated having a son.

Lopeti enjoyed re-telling anecdotes about their little dog, Nita, especially the one about their food bag. When the family left Hihifo, Lopeti remembered seeing the dog on the boat. A boy on the boat dived into the water to retrieve Nita. Later when the boat started to move, Nita jumped out of the boat. 'Aleki was heart-broken at leaving Nita behind. 'Aleki was much relieved when he was told years later by Lopeti via Lute about Nita's life after the family's departure. Lopeti took Nita home to where he lived, in the home of Moahengi and Maletina in Vaipoa. Pesi caught up with Rev Lopeti Taufa in late 2018. Pesi wiped away tears as Rev Lopeti related to her how often he massaged Nita's head when Nita was pining after his missing family.

When Sione's dad, Muni Vaivai, was present, he was quite an entertainer at the frequent kava parties. You would know if he was present from the frequent roar of laughter from the gatherings. If Sione was attending, Muni would use flattery to impress his son.

Fig 119. Rev Lopeti Taufa, Mele Simiki Taufa and Temaleti Vakasioula.

When the boat 'Hifofua' arrived at Niua, Sione always prepared a roast pig and an *'umu* for the 'sailors'. He was grateful to them and was celebrating for their bringing the much needed goods after 6 long months between trips. Sione and Mafi were always very careful with their supplies, ensuring that they did not run out before the next boat arrived.

Lopeti mused that he thoroughly enjoyed Sione and Mafi's company when he was a young man teaching at Vaipoa. He felt very welcomed and loved by both of them.

SHORT LIVES WELL LIVED

Summary:

- Missionaries arrived in Tonga in 1797, and Taufa'ahau, Ruler of Ha'apai, was born.
- Schools established in Hihifo, Tongatapu 1826.
- Rev Egan Moulton arrived to start the secondary school, Tupou College, 1865.
- World War 1, July 1914-Nov 1918.

- Sione Finau Sisifa was born in 1914. Mafi Angahiki Helu was born in 1916.
- They individually made the most of their upbringing to reach their goals in education. On the way, they both became dedicated Christians.
- Sione Finau Sisifa completed his education at the 71 years old Tupou College in 1936. Mafi Helu completed her education at its sister College, Queen Sālote College, two years later in 1938.
- Mafi Angahiki Helu passed away in 1961, aged 45 years old.
- Rev Sione Finau Sisifa passed away in 1969, aged 55 years old.
- This book is written to document their lives and to show their children's respect, admiration and gratefulness to their parents for their lives of love, courage, dedication, and steadfast faith.

Perfect submission, all is at rest,	Si'i Laumalie kuo ne huu:
I in my Saviour am happy and blest;	Hoku loto ni, ke fai hono teu:
Watching and waiting, looking above,	Fakamo'ui hono mahaki,
Filled with His goodness, lost in His love.	Lingi 'ae fiefia 'o langi.
This is my story, this is my song,	Hoku monu e, 'eku koloa,
Praising my Saviour all the day long.	'Eteongo'I he taimi kotoa
This is my story, this is my song,	Fakamo'oni fakapapau
Praising my Saviour all the day long.	Fale 'ae Eiki 'iate au.

FWHB, Tongan Hymn 610, Verse 3. See Page 136 Book By Siupeli T. Taliai

Fig 120. 'Aleki and Latu at our sibling reunion in Suva, Sept 2004.

APPENDICES

Figure Listing

Fig 1. Rev Siupeli and Helen Taliai, 2016.......................... 9

Fig 2. Ha'apai Islands Map 15

Fig 3. Muni-Mata-Mahae story (torn face): The Hercules of the Pacific.. 16

Fig 4. A map of Tonga... 18

Fig 5. Sione Finau Sisifa at Nafualu 1956. 22

Fig 6. Photo of one of the 3 headgears 'Palatavake'. 25

Fig 7. Pesi and Moana admiring the Palatavake displayed at the Madrid American Museum, May 2018. 25

Fig 8. Close-up photo of the 2nd Palatavake.................... 25

Fig 9. The Old Church at Foa. Built 1906, dedicated 1913........... 27

Fig 10. Neomai Helu Taliai. 28

Fig 11. Veitongo School, 1943... 34

Fig 12. A map of Tongatapu... 37

Fig 13. Tafahi as seen from a Niuatoputau beach 40

Fig 14. Tavi and his abode in Tafahi................................ 41

Fig 15. The beach at Lotofoa beyond the 'api 'utas. 46

Fig 16. Evening at Faleloa on Foa Island......................... 47

Fig 17. Fresh food in Lotofoa. 48

Fig 18. Preparing for the Ūloa in Niuatoputapu, with the base of Tafahi visible in the background. 53

Fig 19. Two views of Vai ko Niutoua, Niuatoputapu Island, Tonga. 6 May 2010. 56

Fig 20. The map of Niuatoputapu 58

Fig 21. MV Hifofua @ Taulanga Puatalefusi, Vava'u. 1960.. 59

Fig 22. Wesleyan Church of Hihifo. 63

Fig 23. Sleeping flying foxes in Kolovai. 69

Fig 24. Pesi Fonua's Walking Tour map. 70

Fig 25. At Kolovai [Tongatapu]. l-r: Sione [Latukefu], Teacher Feletoa Vailea, Jan Gammage, Alopi Latukefu. 5 February 1975. 73

Fig 26. The beautiful Kolovai western beach at high tide. 74

Fig 27. The new Kolovai Wesleyan Church (built to the style of the old church). 75

Fig 28. A typical Tongan home in Kolovai in the 1950s. 81

Fig 29. Houma Blowholes 83

Fig 30. Rev Sione Finau and Mafi Helu Sisifa. 83

Fig 31. Sunset on Swimming Beach at Houma. 85

Fig 32. Display at a Langafonua Show. 86

Fig 33. Langafonua. 87

Fig 34. One of the Langafonua Shows. 88

Fig 35. Recent photo of Dr Mele'ana Puloka 89

Fig 36. Nomuka beach. 91

Fig 37. A beach in Lotofoa. 91

Fig 38. THS 1957 Form 2 class in front of the small staff room. .. 92

Fig 39. Queen Salote Wharf 97

Fig 40. Butchering a whale in Ma'ufanga foreshore. 98

Fig 41. Mafi's sister, Meliana Helu Finau. 99

Fig 42. The enlarged, renovated Weslyan Church of Ma'ufanga, November, 2018. 103

Fig 43. Church Women's Group 1958. 106

Fig 44. Yacht mooring at the modern Queen Salote Wharf. 108

Fig 45. Mafi's eldest sister, Numia Taloa 1967. 110

Fig 46. Palu Naulala. 112

Fig. 47. Mele Toa'ila's wedding 7 Sept 1974. 115

Fig 48. Drying newly made tapa cloths. 117

Fig 49. Carrying out the process of tapa making. 118

Fig 50. Pesi receiving her THS Form 5 Academic Award in 1961. 122

Fig 51. 'Aleki receiving his Form 1 Academic Award in 1961 123

Fig 52. Mum and Dad at Fua'amotu Airport in January 1962, farewelling Pesi 127

Fig 53. Japanese boat marooned at a M. reef. 129

Fig 54. A flagstaff on one M. reef. 130

Fig 55. Outside our home in Vaini, Dec 1962. 134

Fig 56. Members of the Vaini Church choir with their Award. 1962.. 134

Fig 57. Rev Sione Finau and his family with the Vaini Church Choir's Cup. 136

Fig 58. Mafi Helu Sisifa's Headstone at Vaini Cemetry. 2017.... 137

Fig 59. 'Ana and Kuli Helu, at their daughter Mele's wedding.... 137

Fig 60. 'Atalanga students 1963.. 138

Fig 61. Mosiana Sisifa, Soana Havea, cousin Sioana Finau with QSC students... 142

Fig 62. Mosiana Sisifa, 1963... 143

Fig 63. Sisi'uno Helu, Futa's mother, at the Fasi parsonage, Jan 1965. 145

Fig 64. Mafi Hingano and Magistrate Hingano Helu seeing Pesi off at the airport, 1965................................ 145

Fig 65. 'Ana and Dr Kuli Helu at the airport 1965. 146

Fig 66. Farewelling Pesi at Fua'amotu Airport, Jan 1965........... 146

Fig 67. Lute started work, 1963.. 147

Fig 68. Newly weds Maeakafa and Lute, 1965 148

Fig 69. Lute at the Nuku'alofa Market, 1965. 149

Fig 70. Futa Helu during the time he was building up 'Atenisi University.. 152

Fig 71. Bryan and Mosiana's wedding in Rosebud, 1965........... 153

Fig 72. Inspector Siaosi Maeakafa Aleamotu'a........................... 155

Fig 73. Lute and Maekafa's finished home. 156

Fig 74. International Students Ball, Auckland University, 1965. Pesi with university staff members. 158

Fig 75i. Siukimoana in Auckland Jan 1970. 159

Fig 75ii. Mele Helu Sisifa with baby Siukimoana 159

Fig 76. Auckland Grammar School Form 6 class, 1966. 160

Fig 77. Last photo of Dad that Mosiana took in 1967. 161

Fig 78. Muni (Viliami Sisifa) and daughter Lilieta at the graveyard of Rev Sione Finau Sisifa 2017............................... 164

Fig 79. Rev C. Gribble (Principal TC), Rev G. Harris (President of Wesleyan Church). 1967. 165

Fig 80. Middle Park, after Sione Na'a's and Diana's wedding, 2009.. 167

Fig 81. Mosiana's family at Wilsons Promontory Oct 2017......... 167

Fig 82. 'Ilaisaane, Mosiana's youngest granddaughter................ 168

Fig 83. Lute and Maeakafa. 1968. 171

Fig 84. Mele Moala, Talimoni, Sulieti Me'a'ofa. April, 2014....... 171

Fig 85. Tangakina and Samuela Fisi'inaua's family, 2006............ 172

Fig 86. Velonika, Tu'ilua, Fa'aseina. 2017.................................. 173

Fig 87. 'Alekisanita Aleamotu'a. August 2018............................ 173

Fig 88. 'Elenoa, Mafi, Fataki, Danielle 'Ilolahia. 15-7-2018........ 174

Fig 89. Lute jr, Fa'aseina Aleamotu'a.2018................................ 175

Fig 90. Argosy Brittania Aleamotu'a, 2015................................ 175

Fig 91. 'Aleki Aleamotua's family.. 175

Fig 92. Moana's admission to the Bar, April 1992. 176

Fig 93. Moana and Marcel, Nov 1996 177

Fig 94. Mafi and Dana, Dec 2001. 177

Fig 95. Mafi and Craig at Moana's wedding, Nov 1996. 178

Fig 96. Lina, Dana, Jordi, March 2017. 179

Fig 97. Siulolo and 'Alekisanita at Setaleki and Belinda's wedding 2012. 181

Fig 98. Palu and Fiona Sisifa with Moana Weir. 2016 181

Fig 99. 'Aleki and his boys, Jan 4th 2013 182

Fig 100. Sione and Sālote Sisifa's family 2018. 183

Fig 101. Mātini and Dinah Sisifa with Princess Pilolevu. 2016.. 184

Fig 102. Mele Teufolau Sisifa 2017. 186

Fig 103. l-r: Dr Latu, Kilisitina, Pesi, Belinda, Setaleki at Dr Steven Sisifa's graduation, ACT 2016. 187

Fig 104. Elizabeth, Nuia and Richmond, 2011 188

Fig 105. Sione Na'a and Diana, 2011. 188

Fig 106. Dr Steven Sisifa at his graduation, 2016 189

Fig 107. Latu and Kilisitina's Family Christmas, 2017 191

Fig 108. 'Aleki, accompanying King Taufa'ahau IV, at the Agricultural Show, Teufaiva Showground 193

Fig 109. 'Aleki with Lord Vaea visiting Rome on business 194

Fig 110. A Tribute to 'Alekisanita Sisifa. author: Co-worker at SPC (South Pacific Community), Fiji 195

Fig 111. At 'Alekisanita's Burial, April, 2014. 196

Fig 112. Unveiling 'Alekisanita's Headstone, April 2015. 196

Fig 113. Dr Palu Sisifa Visits Her Dad's Mala'e After Her Graduation Ceremony In April, 2016. 197

Fig 114. Princess Pilolevu and Lord Tuita were guests of honour. April 2016.. 197

Fig 115. Two Routes For Human Evolution 202

Fig 116. The Polynesian spread of colonizasion throughout the Polynesian Triangle - Kayser 2000, 20008 203

Fig 117. The Moulton Family... 206

Fig 118. Rev. Rodger Page and Queen Sālote during one of her visits to Sydney in the early 1960s..................... 207

Fig 119. Rev Lopeti Taufa, Mele Simiki Taufa and Temaleti Vakasioula. 212

Fig 120. 'Aleki and Latu at our sibling reunion in Suva, Sept 2004... 214

Fig 121. l-r: Pesi, Mele, Lute, Mosiana. Christmas 2017............. 241

Fig 122. Celebrating our first family reunion Sept 2004.............. 241

Fig 123. A family gathering at Edithvale. 242

Fig 124. First Tongan Rugby Team, 1909. Tupou College students, included 3 Helu members... 242

Fig 125. Konai with baby Mafi after Mafi's Christening on June 1971.. 243

Fig 126. l-r: 'Amelia Simiki and 'Akosita Fineanganofo. 243

Fig 127. 'Aleki and Siulolo adoring their first grandchild Viliami, 2001. 244

Fig 128. Mele Lahi Sisifa Helu Latu and daughter Sinitelela, Utah. 2015 244

Fig 129. Latu, Kilisitina with baby Setaleki, Na'a Fiefia at Setaleki's christening in Auckland. 245

Fig 130. Family gathering at Edithvale, Vic. 245

Fig 131. Mosiana's Birthday at Inverloch 2003. 246

Fig 132. 'Ele's graduation celebration dinner, Casino. 246

Fig 133. Mosiana, Siulolo, Aleki, 'Iunisi Fiefia, Bryan. Melb, Jan 2006. 247

Fig 134. Sisifa Siblings at Na'a's wedding, 2011. 247

Fig 135. At the beach house in Somers, VIC, Jan 2015. l-r: Nuia, 'Ele, Steven, Palu, Na'a, Di, Belinda, Setaleki, Alia....... 248

Fig 136. Olive's birthday, May 2016. l-r Lute, Mosiana, Bryan, Mele, Pesi, Latu, Kilisitina.. 248

Fig 137. l-r: Mele, Mosiana, Muni (Viliami) and Pesi at 'Alekisanita's funeral. April, 2014... 249

Fig 138. Pesi's 70th birthday at the Coolart Homestead, Somers. March 2016. back row: l-r Sione Francis, Steven Francis, Argosy Aleamotu'a, Bryan Francis. 2nd row: Helen Skerman, Nicola Evans, Jaki, Moana, Pesi, Mele, Serene Ho, Michael & Georgia Westaway.................................... 249

Fig 139. Farewell dinner for Palu Naulala's family after her funeral at the Melb Casino, July 2016. back row l-r: Simone Ware, Etivina Lovo, Patea Fonua, Kilisitina Sisifa. Linda Manu'atu, Mele Toa'ila Ware, Latu Sisifa, Mosiana Francis, Pesi Weir... 250

Fig 140. Some of the Helu relatives who celebrated Siupeli Taliai's 90th birthday, Feb 2016. 250

Fig. 141. l-r: Cousins Mosiana, Lute, Fatai Fuimaono, Pesi Weir and Mele in Edithvale, Aust. 2018. 251

Fig. 142. Fane Naulala Kite and her family, 2018. l-r: Mana, 'Emeline, Francine, Fane Naulala Kite, Elizabeth, Lord Fatafehi Fakafanua, Lady Fane Fakafanua.......................... 251

Family Tree Listing

FT1. Sione Finau Sisifa: Ancestors 30

FT2. Mafi Angahiki Helu: Ancestors 31

FT3. Taufa Mafile'o Helu's Family Tree.. 120

FT4. Haveahikule'o's Descendents (Helui 1) 139

FT5. Rev Sione F. Sisifa's Ha'afeva Connections 154

FT6. Mosiana (Sisifa) Francis: Descendents................................ 169

FT7. Lute (Sisifa) Aleamotu'a: Descendents 170

FT8. 'Ilisapesi (Sisifa) Weir: Descendents.................................... 180

FT9. 'Alekisanita Uinoaihakau Sisifa: Descendents 185

FT10. Sione Latu Sisifa: Descendents 190

FT11. Rev Tonga Paane Simiki, Rev Sione Finau Sisifa,
Sione Tukia II: Ancestors 229

FT12. Vakasiuola Family Tree.. 229

FT13. Muni's Pelehake family tree... 230

FT14. Muni and Helu with a simplified Tonga Royal Family Tree 231

FT15. Lute and her Aleamotu'a family tree................................. 232

Abbreviations

bro = brother
d = daughter
dc = deceased
gs = grandson
ss = sister
App = Appendices
FT = Family Tree

HGT = History and Geography Of Tonga.
NTT = Niuatoputapu.
QSC = Queen Salote College.
TCSH = Tupou College Sesquicentary History book.

TSQS = Tongan Society At The Time Of Captain Cook by HM Queen Salote, E.Bott, Tavi.
THS = Tonga High School
THSF = Tupou High School, Fasi.
TK = Tu'i Kanokupolu. (Tu'i means King)
TP = Tu'i Pelehake.
TT = Tu'i Tonga

Memories of Sione Finau Sisifa in the 1930 by Sela Tafisi, 79 years old (dc)
15 June 2004

Ko Sione mo Mafi na'a na maheni pe'i Pelehake. Ko Sione na'e ma'unga nofo ange pe ki Pelehake he taimi tutuku 'ae ako. Koe fa'e 'a Muni Vaivai 'a ia koe kui ia 'a Sione mo Tevita, ko Heulupe mei Pelehake, na'e mali mo Muni mei Lofanga. Na'e 'i ai 'ae fu'u fale kapa lahi na'e nofo ai 'a e fa'e tangata 'a Muni Vaivai ko Sione Taufa pea na'e nofo ai 'a Muni pehē ki he tamaiki 'i he tutuku 'ae ako. Koe fale ni foki 'o 'enau kui ko Fatafehi Toutai Tokotaha na'e ta'ane mo Fusipala. Ko Sione Taufa na'e ngāue fakafaifekau pea koia na'e sai'ia 'ia Mafi ke mali mo Sione ko 'ene faka'ofo'ofa mo anga māu. Ko Muni Vaivai koe kaunga tangata ia 'o Tungi Mailefihi, pea na'a na fa'a nofo pe 'i Pelehake. Koe fu'u famili ofi ia 'o Tungi Mailefihi, 'a Muni.

Koe Tupufakaholo 'o Muni, Kui 'a Sione Finau Sisifa 'i he manatu 'a Sela Tafisi Liava'a

Koe tupu'anga 'o Heulupe fa'e 'a Muni Vaivai ko Levao. koe foha 'eve'eva 'o e Tu'ipelehake ko Fatafehi Toutai Tokotaha (TP IV). Na'e ta'ane 'a Fatafehi Toutai Tokotaha mo Fusipala Tauki'onetuku (koe 'ofefine 'oe Pilinisi Kalauni mo Palemia ko Tevita 'Unga) 'o 'i ai 'a Tu'i Siaosi Tupou II.

Ko Fatafehi Toutai (TP IV) koe foha ia 'oe Tu'ipelehake ko Filiaipulotu (TP III) koe foha ia 'o'Uluvalu koe Tu'ipelehake II, koe foha 'o Lekaumoana, (TP I). Verified on Fig 24 TSQS, page 78.

Na'e mali 'a Levao pea mo Vaihū 'o 'i ai 'a e fanau ko 'eni: Ko Fonise (f); Lavinia (f); Kafo'atu (f); Ma'ata (f); Heulupe (f); Sione Taufa (m) ; Sione Filipe (m).

Na'e mali 'a e ta'ahine lahi,'a Fonise kia Paula Kolongahau 'o 'i ai 'a e ta'ahine pē 'e tokotaha ko Katokakala koe fa'ē ia 'a Sela Tafisi. Na'e mali 'a Katokakala ki Ha'avakatolo kia Semisi Liava'a (hako 'o 'Uhilamoelangi 'a Haveahikule'o pea mo Halaevalu Fonongava'inga, Mumui's daughter).

Na'e pehee 'e Sela na'e 'ofa 'aupito 'a 'ene fa'ē 'ia Muni mo 'ene fanau. Ko e mehikitanga 'o Katokakala ko Mele Sisifa, koe tuofefine 'o 'ene tamai (Paula Kolongahau). Na'e pusiaki'i 'e Mele Sisifa 'a Muni Vaivai. Ko Mele Sisifa 'i he talanoa 'a Sela na'e 'ikai ke mali ka koe fefine na'e nima malohi he ngāue ki he koloa fakatonga, pea na'e pusiaki fanau tokolahi foki.

Na'e mali leva 'a e kau fefine: 'a Lavinia kia 'Aisea Manumu'a, Kafo'atu na'e mali ia ki Niutoua, pea ko Ma'ata na'e mali mo Lafumoa. Ko Heulupe na'e mali ia kia Muni mei Lofanga 'o 'iai 'a Muni Vaivai. Na'e mali 'a Muni Vaivai ki Ha'afeva kia Uaafe 'o 'iai 'a Sione mo Tevita. Ko Sione Taufa na'e ngaue fakafaifekau 'i he Siasi Tonga Tau'ataina, pea ko Sione Filipe Tongailava na'e mali mo Funaki koe tehina 'o Maikale Taumoepenu 'o 'iai 'a Liu Tongilava, Maketi Tongilava etc.

(Na'e pehē 'e Sione Finau Sisifa 'i he 'ene tohi faka'osi kia Pesi, ko Funaki Tongilava mo Maikale Taumoepenu na'a na tamai taha mo fa'e taha mo Muni Vaivai?)

Na'e 'i ai foki moe fefine Lofanga, nofo Pelehake (na'e faka'osi nofo 'i Kolomotu'a) ko Ane. Na'e mali 'a Ane moe Matapule ko Ikahihifo. Na'a ne fakamatala 'ae me'a tatau moe fakahohoko 'e Sela Tafisi. Na'e pehē 'e Ane na'e fekau 'e Kuini Sālote ki he'ene fa'e ke 'alu ki he 'api 'o Lute mo Maeakafa mo ha koloa ki he mohenga 'o si'i tangata'eiki faifekau. Pea ne 'afio ange kenau tokanga ki he tangata'eiki he 'oku mahamahaki.

English version of this story:

Lute found out about our Dad's Pelehake connections from Sela Tafisi in 2004, when Sela Tafisi lived in Kolomotu'a and frequented the Palace to wait on the Royal family. According to Sela Tafisi, our grandad (Viliami) Muni's forebears came from Pelehake originally.

Sela's explanation of Dad's origin and his Pelehake connections are as shown in the family trees,

The Pelehake story was backed by another Pelehake/Lofanga woman named Ane who was married to a Matapule called Ikahihifo.

Ane Ikahihifo was also living in Kolomotu'a in 2004. She told Lute that her mum was sent by HM Queen Sālote to take some tapa cloth and mats to our Dad when he was incapacitated. Queen Salote also asked Ane's mum to watch out for our Dad as he was not well.

FT 11 does not match exactly with the brief ancestry diagram Dad pencilled for Pesi. It has baffled the siblings that they have no stories about other Munis except the Legendry Muni-mata-mahae.

Dad, in his note to Pesi before he passed away, wrote that Maikale Taumoepenu and Funaki Tongilava were his aunties. They had the same mother and father as his dad!? There are anomalies here, which can be the result of having close relatives living together under one roof. Their children can be confused themselves who their real parents were.

Lute and Pesi cannot confirm Sela's and Ane's full stories but much of them dovetail with what they know about grandad and Dad. They know that their grandfather (Viliami) Muni spent a lot of time in Pelehake as described by Sela Tafisi and Ane Ikahihifo, when quite young as well as when he was working at the 'Utulau gardens with the Prince Consort Tungi Mailefihi.

FT11. Rev Tonga Paane Simiki, Rev Sione Finau Sisifa, Sione Tukia II: Ancestors

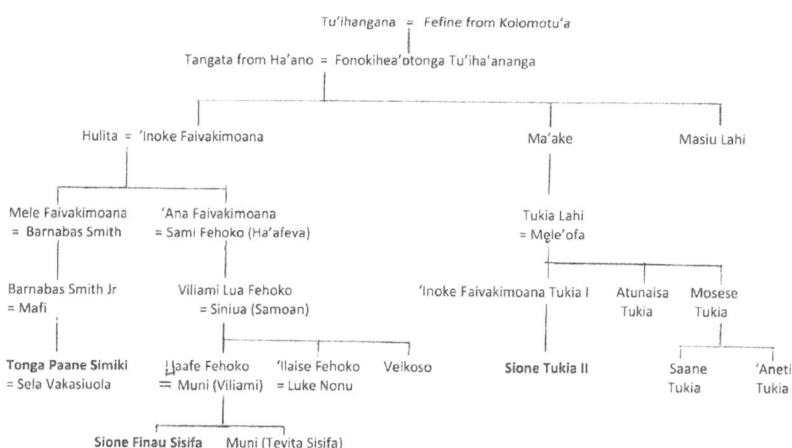

FT12. Vakasiuola Family Tree

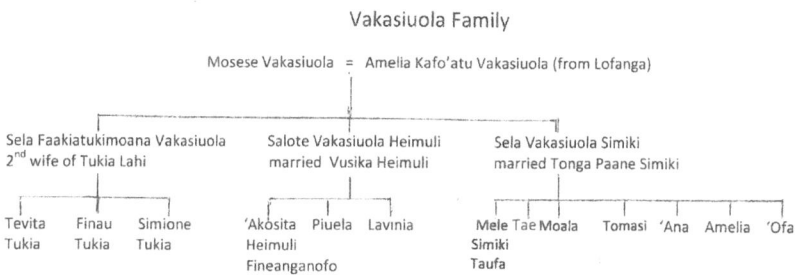

FT13. Muni's Pelehake family tree.

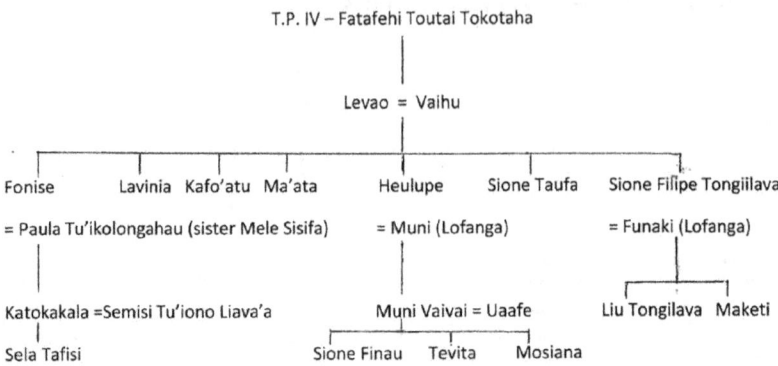

FT14. Muni and Helu with a simplified Tonga Royal Family Tree.

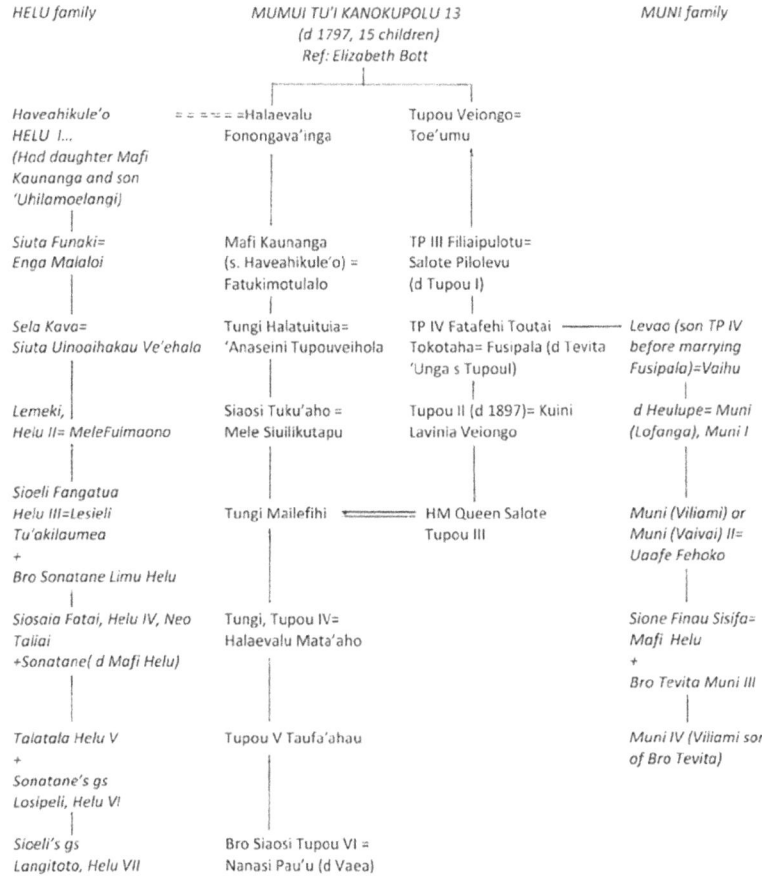

FT15. Lute and her Aleamotu'a family tree.

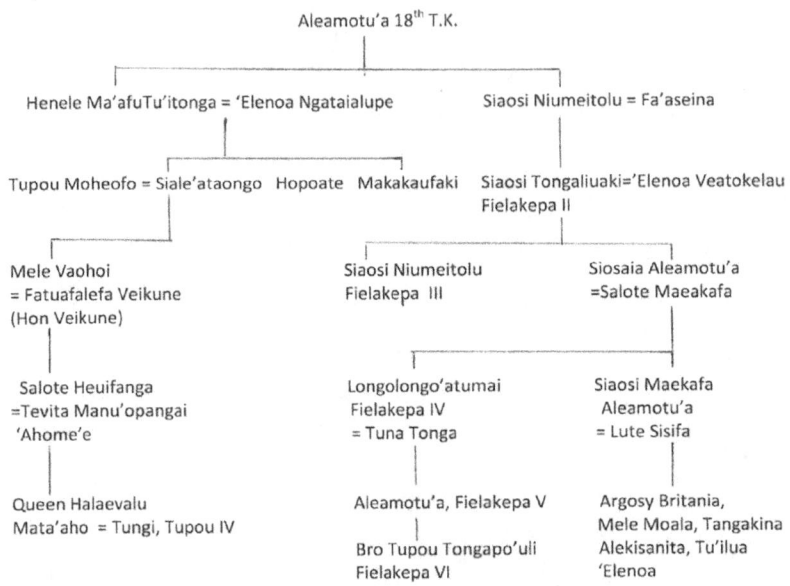

TALES FROM THE KINGDOM OF TONGA

KO E KI`I KOLO KAKALA.

Ko e Tohi `a S.F.Sisifa, Vaipoa- `Okatopa, 1951.

Fakamolemole pe `a e ngaahi ha`a `oku kau ki he Kolo Kakala `ilongaa, na`a ngali kuo fakatataua mei tokelau mama`o `a e hingoa tuha mo ia kuo tau nofo`aki mai talu fuoloa. `Oku `ikai ko ha founga pehe, ka ko `eni pe `e haa atu.

`Oku tu`u `a Tafahi ki he tokelau `o Niua Toputapu. Ko e motu mo`unga ia pea `oku ne hoko pe ki Kao `i he ma`olunga taha `i Tonga ni. `Oku tu`u foki hono ki`i koloo `i he tokelau pea ko ha tafungofunga ki `olunga `o `ikai si`i hifo `i he fute `e 50 hono ma`olunga mei he tahi.

`I he te`eki `a`ahi mai `a e ongo papalangi na`e fua sio ki he konga `o Tonga ni he ta`u 1616 kuo fuoloa hono nofo`i `a e ki`i kolo ni ko e kakai tukuhau `oku nofo ai he taimi ni `oku `ikai si`i hifo he 20. `Oku tatau mo `Utulau `a e lahi `o e kolo ni, ka e ma`opo`opo pe `a e nofo`i `o e kolo ni.

`Oku nau mo`ui lelei tu`unga ki he`ene `ea lelei pea kelekele mo`ui `aupito `a e motu `o `aonga `aupito ki he ngouee pea faka`ulia foki ko e tupu noa`ia ai `a e ngaahi `akau fua `aonga ki he tokoni, pea `oku ne meimei fua hokohoko pe mo fua `aonga ki he tokoni pea mo fua lahi `aupito, pea `oku kau `a e motu ni ki he Kalasi `uluaki `i he tu`umalie he me`a tokonii ma`u aipe.

Kuo fuoloa moe fifili `a Mosese Vaka (Ko e `Eiki `o e Koloo ki ha hingoa fe`unga mo hono ki`i kolo `i Tafahii, faifai na`a ne fakapapau`i ke fakahingoa leva, pea `i he `aho 6 `o Sanuali, 1946, na`a ne ui leva ko *KOLOKAKALA `O FUNGA FAONO*

`E fakalongolongo`i pe `a e Fungafaono he ko e fakamanatu pe ia ki he ta`u na`e fakahingoa aii, kau ui pe `a e Kolokakala.

`I he kelekele mo`ui `a e kolo ni kuo to ai mo tupu noa`ia aipe `a e fa`ahinga kakala kehekehe pe `o ne mo`ui vave pea matala pe mo fua kei iiki pea to e `i ai foki mo e `akau namu kakala ko e fue `oku fai lolo `aki, pea hei`ilo pe `oku toe `i ha feitu`u `i Tonga ni pe `ikai. Ko konga pe ia `oku sio ki ai `a e hingoa ni.

`Oku lahi `etau ngaahi ngaue `oku ngaue`aki `a e kakala ni ka ko hono ngaue`aki ki he kahoaa `oku mau fie to`o hakee pea mau fakalave ai foki mo e kahoa puekii he `oku tefito `a e puekii ki Tafahi, pea kuo lahi hono ngaue`aki `i Tonga ni ka e `uma`a hono manakoa mei muli, pea pehee foki mo e kahoa koeni.

`Oku `ikai ha hosi `i motu ni pea ko e `akau ha`amo tokonaki `oku ui ko e hosi. `Oku tauhi he `api kotoape `a e hosi `akau `e 2 pe lahi hake kuo `osi ngaohi fakalelei`i pea `oku nau kahoa mei mo`unga he `aho kotoa pe `a e fa`ahinga tokonaki kehekehe pe, pea ko e ngahi founga ni kuo ui ai `a e ki`i kolo `o Tafahi ko e Kolokakala.

Kau Akolotu feinga'i hotau loto ke kelekele tau ki he tuutuu'i 'a e tenga mo'ui 'o e 'ofa, tui, 'amanaki, kataki, angamaluu, fiefakamolemole etc, pea hei'ilo 'e tupu hake 'o matala pea 'alaha, pea fie teunga mo ngaue'aki kitaua 'e he fonua, kolo, famili, kae'uma'a hotau Siasi, pea 'e tonu ke ui 'a e ngaahi loto pehe ko e Kolokakala 'o ui pehe 'i he potu kotoape 'e 'iloa ai koe.

Pea ko e fa'ahinga kolo ia 'oku lata ki ai 'a e 'Eikii 'o fakaivi'i mo tala fatongia mei ai. Hangee tofu pe ko e lau 'a e Himi 510 veesi *Loto mo e 'atamai; Ko ho Pule'anga ia; Fokotu'u taloni ai; Tala ai ho fatongia"

<u>Pea koe naanaafaki 'a e fa'ahinga kakala 'oku toli ke teunga'aki 'i he kolo 'oku te'eki si'i haa mai</u>.

Letter 2. From Vaipoa

Dear Ismuella Heyward.   Vaipoa, Niuatoputapu 9th March 45.

In February 24th I received your letter. It was very interested to us. In your letter shows us that you were wondering if I had received the parcel of books. I already got them all last year, my word! They are very helpful in my work and in our personal life. One of them named "My Witnesses" I use to say it is the most important of all the books I have got.

If you got a map of the Tongan islands, you must know where we are now. It is a very hot island.

I have told you I will send you something for a present in January but I am sorry to say that the boat did not come from Tongatapu in that month. Here are they. Two string of beads which made with shells called PUEKI. I think they are not interested for you but you may hang them up in your study as a little remembrance for myself in this far island. We believe that the war will be over so soon, and it will be a good day for you and your family, also the millions of people in many different places of the world, who are staying far from their own homes and families because the war. May God gives His own mercy upon you and your family, and save you and us all while these hard days.

We are very glad to hear that you still remember many things while we were in Veitongo Tongatapu. We brought Draughts and Chineese Checkers. We use to play both of them here.

There are two districts in this island. Hihifo & Vaipoa, and I have two villages in my district and one island. There is no school in my district then Mr Page told me to establish school in Vaipoa. so I am ready to be started on June, but I was preparing four men in this island for the entrance examination for the Theological School. The examination was held in the church on 5 & 6 inst. I hope they will all pass. Two men from Hihifo, one in our own village and one man from Falehau (another village)

Hafi and I are really working hard in preparing many lessons in Sunday School. We will have a big ceremony in the first Sunday of May, we wish you would come over and see it.

When the school start in June we will take a concert as we took in Veitongo. We will take this in enclosing school in December.

We got the parcel of books very soon, because all the men in the Post Office know me, and whenever the parcels reached, they exchanged my address into Vaipoa, Niua Toputapu and sent it over.

Last year the Government of Tonga sent us flour, sugar, jam, B.Powder, Biscuits, Salmon, Soups, Blue, because we are having every sort of food and money when the hurricane visited the island and destroyed all the food puddings and coconut trees. In the new year the chiefs and the people begged me to write a little to the Queen and the Government and asking them to let them free from polltax and to give clothes too, so I did it for them.

I have told Mr Page that you have sent me books + he was happy too. Mr Page always send me weekly news in every boat. I suppose he will be happy if you can write him a little letter.

> On Wednesday night of this week we took a little party of Rosiana's birthday. We talked about you at that night. She is growing very quickly and she knows many words, and she can talk a little. I use to save these two dozen stamps for you, one dozen is the Queen's jubilee, and another dozen is the National tree in the Government's playground at Nuku'alofa.
>   I enclosing this letter with great love to you all.
>   From Sione Finau Sisifa.
> Love from Kafi to you and all your family.

The Legend of Munimatamahae of Lofanga, The Hercules of the Pacific

There are many versions of this myth or legend. Tupou Posesi Fanua, Dr Posesi Fanua's wife, published a collection of Tongan legends in 1975 called 'Po Fananga'. NZ author, Robert Craig, in 'The Handbook of Polynesian Mythology', tells the closest story to that which my Dad related to me.

Long time ago, there lived a young couple, Motukuve'evalu (swamp dwelling 8-legged hen) and his wife Kae, in the eastern end of Tongatapu. There also lived a wicked vicious chief in this vicinity called Pungalotohoa. The couple laid low, hiding in the bush away from their wicked chief. When Kae became pregnant, her husband Motukuve'evalu, made plans for her to travel back to her parents in Ha'apai for her and their baby's safety. To their misfortune, the next boat to Ha'apai was owned by no other than Pungalotohoa. In spite of this, Kae set out with her belongings on her voyage to Ha'apai with many other passengers. Enemies of Motukuve'evalu recognised Kae on the boat. They set upon her, murdered her, ripped her unborn baby out of her body and chucked them both overboard.

The abandoned baby survived the elements and reached the shores of a little island called Lofanga. Days after, a fisherman and his wife found the baby, with one eye torn and bruised from being pecked by seabirds. The couple took the baby home and brought him up like their very own. The boy grew fast and became a big strong young man. Everyone was astounded by his strength and feats. He was known to push a coconut tree to the ground for example. Some villagers became very envious of the young lad and even feared him. A plan was hatched to get rid of him. In the next community meeting, it was decided that Muni was to carry out few very difficult tasks. If he failed any one of them, he and his parents would be executed or at best, banished to a faraway land.

The first task was to weave half of a big communal fishing net, while the rest of the community would weave the remaining half. Muni asked his parents to leave it to him. He completed his task very easily. The second task was harder. He and his parents were to build half of a fence around the communal mala'e (marae) while the rest of the community complete the other half. Muni-matamahae completed this task easily without his parents. The third task was so hard that when Muni completed it, the community could not believe their eyes. He and his family were to build an outrigger, complete with a hut for it in 2 days. Muni set to, felling trees, gathering materials and completing these tasks in the set time. When he finished, the rest of the community were still collecting their building materials and arguing about how to go about doing their tasks.

Yet another task was thought up. Muni and his parents were told to watch over a communal canoe that was anchored at the beach at night. While the family were asleep in the boat, villagers drilled holes on the side of the boat, cut the rope anchoring it and pushed the boat out to sea. When Muni awoke and saw their predicament, he bailed the water out of the leaking boat with a coconut shell and rowed their boat swiftly with a plank of wood from the side of the boat. They went in the direction of the trade wind and they finally landed in an island in Fiji. During the night, Muni overheard his parents talking about how much they loved their son and how he had developed from the baby they found on the beach years ago. Muni sat up and demanded that they tell him all about his origin. They told him everything, about his father in Tongatapu, and how he hides in the bush from the wicked vicious chief. They told him that it was time he went and rescued his father. They gave him detailed instructions on how to find him.

Muni set out to find his father, Motukuve'evalu. When they met, they embraced for a long time. His father then went off to search for food. Muni decided to clear the trees around the land in preparation for growing more yams. He then lit a fire to cook food. On Motukuve'evalu return he viewed the cleared land with fear in his heart. Now he had no protection against the wicked chief and the smoke would alert the vicious chief of his whereabouts. The next day, Muni went to seek out and confront Pungalotohoa. He found that the chief was not in his big 'fale'. He tore the chief's gate down, ripped out his precious kava plants, roots and all. On his return, Pungalotohoa was enraged and challenged Muni to a throwing contest and a boxing match. Punga's strength was no match to Muni's. Muni's spear disappeared into the blue sky. In the final challenge, Pungalotohoa collapsed.

Before he died, he gave all his possessions, land, his wives and even his title to Muni. Muni next collected his father and his relatives from the bush, to live in their new home, in safety and peace. He became a loving ruler. Everyone lived happily ever after.

PHOTOS

Fig 121. l-r: Pesi, Mele, Lute, Mosiana. Christmas 2017. With baby Mafi 'Ilolahia and baby 'Ilaisaane Francis.

Fig 122. Celebrating our first family reunion Sept 2004. back row l-r: 'Aleki jr, 'Aleki Sr, Bryan, Sione F. Sisifa, 2nd row: Mele, Lute, Mosiana, Pesi, front row: Viliami, Salote, Kilisitina, Siulolo.

Fig 123. A family gathering at Edithvale. back row. l-r: Pesi, Lute, Bryan, Helen, Tina. 2nd row: Mele, Mosiana, Siupeli, Latu. 3rd row Jaki, Sione, 'Elenoa, Lesieli & Sione Taufa. front row: Tama & AliaFrancis, Danielle 'Ilolahia, Mia Taufa. Jan 2014.

Fig 124. First Tongan Rugby Team, 1909. Tupou College students, included 3 Helu members: Dad Sioeli, son Fatai, son 'Ofa.

Fig 125. Konai with baby Mafi after her Christening on June 1971.

Fig 126. l-r: 'Amelia Simiki and 'Akosita Fineanganofo.

Fig 127. 'Aleki and Siulolo adoring their first grandchild Viliami, 2001.

Fig 128. Mele Lahi Sisifa Helu Latu and daughter Sinitelela, Utah. 2015.

Fig 129. Latu, Kilisitina with baby Setaleki, Na'a Fiefia at Setaleki's christening in Auckland.

Fig 130. back row. l-r: Titian, Steven, Michelle, Michael, Sione, Jaki, Moana, Dana, 'Isi Bryan, Pesi, Lute, Helen, Siupeli, Mosiana, Ron. front row: Mele, Lina. 2001

Fig 131. Mosiana's Birthday at Inverloch 2003. Back row: l-r Titian, Na'a Sione, Michelle, Michae, Marcel. 2nd row: Steven, Latu, Mele, Lina, Pesi, Lute, Mosiana, Jaki. front: Steven, 'Isi Bryan, Dana, Tina.

Fig 132. 'Ele's graduation celebration dinner, Casino.
l-r: Latu Sisifa, Pesi Weir, Mele Sisifa, Lute Aleamotu'a, Danielle 'Ilolahia Kilisitina Sisifa, Mosiana Franacis, Bryan Francis, Fataki 'Ilolahia, 'Elenoa Aleamotu'a 'Ilolahia.

Fig 133. Mosiana, Siulolo, Aleki, 'Iunisi Fiefia, Bryan. Melb, Jan 2006.

Fig 134. Sisifa Siblings at Na'a Sisifa's wedding, 2011.

Fig 135. At the beach house in Somers, VIC, Jan 2015. l-r: Nuia, 'Ele Steven, Palu, Na'a Di, Belinda, Setaleki, Alia.

Fig 136. Olive's birthday, May 2016. l-r Lute, Mosiana, Bryan, Mele, Pesi, Latu, Kilisitina.

Fig 137. l-r: Mele, Mosiana, Muni (Viliami) and Pesi at 'Alekisanita's funeral. April, 2014.

Fig 138. Pesi's 70th birthday at the Coolart Homestead, Somers. March 2016. back row: l-r Sione Francis, Steven Francis, Argosy Aleamotu'a Bryan Francis. 2nd row: Helen Skerman, Nicola Evans, Jaki, Moana, Pesi, Mele, Serene Ho, Michael & Georgia Westaway.

Fig 139. Farewell dinner for Palu Naulala's family after her funeral at the Melb Casino, July 2016. back row l-r: Simone Ware, 'Etivina Lovo, Patea Fonua, Kilisitina Sisifa. Linda Manu'atu Mele Toa'ila Ware, Latu Sisifa, Mosiana Francis, Pesi Weir.

Fig 140. Some of the Helu relatives who celebrated Siupeli Taliai's 90th birthday, Feb 2016. back row: Jeff Helu, Leisi Helu, Susana Helu, Mele Fifita Hausia, Fangumapa, Siosaia Fangaloka, Suli Helu, Haveahikule'o, 'Ikani Taliai, Manutu'ufanga Naufahu. 2nd row: Lute, Pesi, Mosiana, Lesieli sr, Pasemata Ve'ehala Taunisila, Siupeli with Layla, Helen with Jordyn, Ben Naufahu.

Fig. 141. l-r: Cousins Mosiana, Lute, Fatai Fuimaono, Pesi Weir and Mele in Edithvale, Aust. 2018.

Fig. 142. Fane Naulala Kite and her family, 2018.
l-r: Mana, 'Emeline, Francine, Fane Naulala Kite, Elizabeth, Lord Fatafehi Fakafanua, Lady Fane Fakafanua.

www.ingramcontent.com/pod-product-compliance
Lightning Source LLC
LaVergne TN
LVHW021658060526
838200LV00050B/2402